AQA Religious Studies B

Religion and Citizenship

GCSE

Marianne Fleming
Anne Jordan
Peter Smith
David Worden

Series editor
Cynthia Bartlett

Nelson Thornes

Text © Marianne Fleming, Anne Jordan, Peter Smith and David Worden 2009

Original illustrations © Nelson Thornes Ltd 2009

The right of Marianne Fleming, Anne Jordan, Peter Smith and David Worden to be identified as the authors of this work has been asserted by them in accordance with the Copyright, Designs and Patents Act 1988.

All rights reserved. No part of this publication may be reproduced or transmitted in any form or by any means, electronic or mechanical, including photocopy, recording or any information storage and retrieval system, without permission in writing from the publisher or under licence from the Copyright Licensing Agency Limited, of Saffron House, 6–10 Kirby Street, London, EC1N 8TS.

Any person who commits any unauthorised act in relation to this publication may be liable to criminal prosecution and civil claims for damages.

Published in 2009 by:
Nelson Thornes Ltd
Delta Place
27 Bath Road
CHELTENHAM
GL53 7TH
United Kingdom

12 13 / 10 9 8 7 6 5

A catalogue record for this book is available from the British Library

ISBN 978 1 4085 0512 0

Cover photograph/illustration by Alamy/ Jupiter Images/ Brand X

Illustrations by AMR Design

Page make-up by AMR Design, (www.amrdesign.com)

Printed by Multivista Global Ltd

Photo Acknowledgements

Alamy: Brian Parkes / 1.5A; Chuck Nacke / 3.2B; Image100 / 4.1A; INTERFOTO Pressebildagentur / 2.8B; Janine Wiedel Photolibrary / 4.1B; Photodisc / 5.11A; Photofusion Picture Library / 4.11A; **Corbis:** Alexandra Winkler / Reuters / 3.10A; Bob Krist / 1.6A; Christopher Morris / 2.9B; **Catholics for Choice:** 1.4A; **CND:** 6.6A; **David Worden:** 4.8A; **Fotolia:** 1.1B; 1.10B; 1.11A; 2.1A; 2.1B; 2.1C; 2.2A; 2.3D; 2.4A; 2.4B; 2.4C; 2.5A; 2.5B; 2.5C1; 2.5C2; 2.6A; 2.6B; 2.10A; 2.10B; 2.10C; 2.11A; 3.1A; 3.1B; 3.2C; 3.3A; 3.4A; 3.5A; 3.5B; 3.5C; 3.6A; 3.6B; 3.7A; 3.8A; 3.8B; 3.9A; 3.10B; 3.11A; 4.4A; 4.5B; 4.6A; 5.2A; 5.2B; 5.3A; 5.3B; 5.4A; 5.4B; 5.5A; 5.6A; 5.6B; 5.7C; 5.8B; 5.9A; 5.9B; 5.10A; 6.1A; 6.1B; 6.7A; 6.8B; 6.10A; 6.10B; 6.11A; **Geoff Covey:** 2.8A; **Getty Images:** 2.3A; Tim Graham / 4.5A; **iStockphoto:** 1.2A; 1.3B; 1.7B; 1.8A; 1.8B; 1.9A; 2.2B; 2.3B; 2.3C; 2.4D; 2.9A; 3.1C; 3.3B; 3.4B; 3.7B; 3.7C; 4.2A; 4.2B; 4.3A; 4.3B; 4.4B; 4.7A; 4.8B; 4.8C; 4.9A; 4.9B; 4.9C; 4.10A; 4.10B; 4.10C; 5.1A; 5.4C; 5.7A; 5.7B; 5.8A; 6.2A; 6.2B; 6.3A; 6.3B; 6.4A; 6.4B; 6.8A; 6.9A; 6.9B; **Lifeway Church Resources:** 1.3A; **PA Photos:** AP / 6.7B; John Giles / 2.7A; **Rex Features:** Israel Images / 1.6B; Jonathan Hordle / 6.5A; **Samaritans:** 6.5B; **St Stephen's Society:** 3.2A.

Text Acknowledgements

Scripture quotations taken from the Holy Bible, New International Version. Copyright © 1978, 1984 by International Bible Society. Used by permission of Hodder & Stoughton, a division of Hodder Headline Ltd. All rights reserved. "NIV" is a registered trademark of International Bible Society. UK trademark number 1448790.

1.1: Reprinted with permission of the Church of England Liturgical Commission.
2.1: Short quote from 'Notes of a Painter, 1908' Translation from 'Matisse on Art' by Jack Flam, revised edition 1995. © Succession Henri Matisse. Reprinted with permisison
2.7: Quote by the International Olympic Committee. Reprinted with permission.
2.10: Short quote by Nelson Mandela, 1994. Reprinted with permission.
2.10, 5.2, 5.8 & 6.8: Extracts from THE HOLY QURAN TRANSLATION AND COMMENTARY by Abdullah Yusuf Ali. Reprinted with permission of IPCI – Islamic Vision, 434 Coventry Road, Small Heath, Birmingham B10 0UG UK.
3.5: Crown Copyright materials reproduced with permission of the controller of the HMSO.
4.5: Short extract from marriage ceremony – Archbishop's Council 2000, and the oath of loyalty made by Bishops. Reprinted with permission of Church House Publishing.
5.3: Short extract from THE ROMAN CATHOLIC CATECHISM, Burns and Oates. English translation for United Kingdom Copyright © 1974, 1999 Burns & Oates – Libreria Editrice Vaticana. Reprinted by permission of Continuum International Publishing Group UK.
6.3, 6.6 & 6.7: EXTRACTS from The Universal Declaration of Human Rights. Reprinted with permission of United Nations.
6.4: Short ChildLine quote. Reprinted with permission.
6.8: Quote by Nobel Committee at the giving of the Nobel Peace Prize in 1989 to Dalai Lama. Reprinted with permission.
6.10: Short extract from 'I Have a Dream Speech' by Dr. Martin Luther King Jr. Reprinted by arrangement with The Heirs to the Estate of Martin Luther King Jr., c/o Writers House as agent for the proprietor New York, NY Copyright © 1963 Dr. Martin Luther King Jr; Copyright renewed 1991 Coretta Scott King.

Contents

Introduction 5

1 Religion and relationships 8
1.1 Relationships 8
1.2 Sexual relationships 10
1.3 Sex before marriage 12
1.4 Religious attitudes to contraception 14
1.5 The purpose and character of marriage 16
1.6 Religious weddings 18
1.7 Choices 20
1.8 Being a good parent 22
1.9 Sex outside marriage 24
1.10 Divorce 26
Chapter 1: Assessment guidance 28

2 Religion, sport and leisure 30
2.1 Stress and relaxation 30
2.2 Leisure 32
2.3 Benefits of leisure 34
2.4 Misuse of leisure 36
2.5 Religion and sport 38
2.6 Morality in sport 40
2.7 Performance-enhancing drugs 42
2.8 Sports fans 44
2.9 Support within sport and leisure 46
2.10 Issues of equality 48
Chapter 2: Assessment guidance 50

3 Religion and work 52
3.1 The purpose and importance of work 52
3.2 Careers and vocation 54
3.3 Business and enterprise 56
3.4 The economy and taxation 58
3.5 Rights and responsibilities: employers 60
3.6 Rights and responsibilities: employees 62
3.7 Trade unions 64
3.8 Voluntary work and service 66
3.9 The work of religious voluntary organisations 68
3.10 Unemployment and the value of work 70
Chapter 3: Assessment guidance 72

4 Religion and the multicultural society 74
4.1 Multiculturalism 74
4.2 Living in a multicultural society 76
4.3 Advantages and disadvantages of multiculturalism 78
4.4 Religion and politics 80
4.5 State religion and blasphemy laws 82
4.6 Immigration 84
4.7 Asylum seekers, integration and faith communities 86
4.8 Faith communities 88
4.9 Wesak, Christmas and Diwali 90
4.10 Eid-ul-Fitr, Pesach and Baisakhi 92
Chapter 4: Assessment guidance 94

5 Religion and identity — 96

- 5.1 Who am I? — 96
- 5.2 The value and importance of human life — 98
- 5.3 The spiritual dimension of life — 100
- 5.4 Has life got meaning and purpose? — 102
- 5.5 Image and views of 'self' — 104
- 5.6 Identity within faith communities (1) — 106
- 5.7 Identity within faith communities (2) — 108
- 5.8 Symbolism and dress — 110
- 5.9 Healthy living and sacred writings — 112
- 5.10 Interdependence and decision making — 114

Chapter 5: Assessment guidance — 116

6 Religion and human rights — 118

- 6.1 Rights and responsibilities — 118
- 6.2 Religious attitudes towards the law and human rights — 120
- 6.3 Human rights legislation — 122
- 6.4 Children's rights and support — 124
- 6.5 Citizen's Advice and the Samaritans — 126
- 6.6 Pressure groups — 128
- 6.7 Forms of protest — 130
- 6.8 Religions and protest — 132
- 6.9 Religious protests and support for non-religious campaigning organisations — 134
- 6.10 Religious campaigners who support human rights — 136

Chapter 6: Assessment guidance — 138

Glossary — 140

Index — 143

Nelson Thornes and AQA

Nelson Thornes has worked in partnership with AQA to make sure that this book offers you the best possible support for your GCSE course. All the content has been approved by the senior examining team at AQA, so you can be sure that it gives you just what you need when you are preparing for your exams.

■ How to use this book

This book covers everything you need for your course.

Learning Objectives

At the beginning of each section or topic you'll find a list of Learning Objectives based on the requirements of the specification, so you can make sure you are covering everything you need to know for the exam.

Objectives
Objectives
Objectives
Objectives

First objective.

Second objective.

AQA Examiner's Tips

Don't forget to look at the AQA Examiner's Tips throughout the book to help you with your study and prepare for your exam.

> **AQA Examiner's tip**
>
> Don't forget to look at the AQA Examiner's Tips throughout the book to help you with your study and prepare for your exam.

AQA Examination-style Questions

These offer opportunities to practise doing questions in the style that you can expect in your exam so that you can be fully prepared on the day.

AQA examination questions are reproduced by permission of the Assessment and Qualifications Alliance.

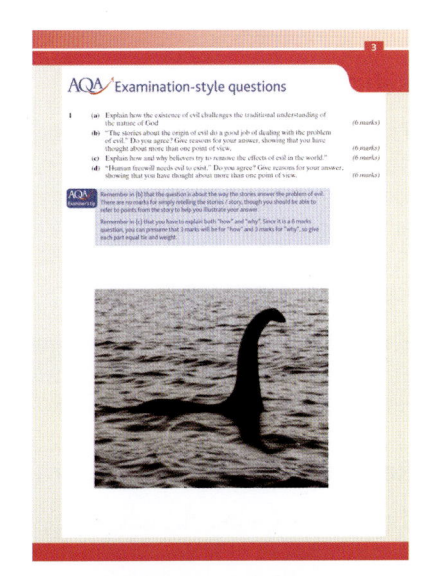

www.nelsonthornes.com/aqagcse

AQA GCSE Religion and Citizenship

This book is written for GCSE students studying the AQA Religious Studies Specification B, Unit 1: Religion and Citizenship. You are encouraged to consider religion and citizenship, including relationships, the need for work and leisure, multiculturalism, identity and human rights. The specification allows for the study solely of Buddhism, Christianity, Hinduism, Islam, Judaism or Sikhism, or for a combination of any of these religions.

You do not have to be religious to study this course, but it will enable you to develop your knowledge, skills and understanding of religion. You will have the opportunity to study the significance and impact of certain aspects of the religions. You will have the chance to express personal opinions and gain informed insights on some fundamental questions and issues.

■ Topics in this unit

In the examination you will be asked to answer four questions, based on four of the following six topics:

Religion and relationships

This topic examines human sexuality and sexual relationships, and the purpose and character of marriage.

Religion, sport and leisure

This topic examines religious attitudes towards the purpose, use and importance of sport and leisure. It looks at morality in sport, the devotion of fans and at the pay of superstars.

Religion and work

This topic links with work experience, business and enterprise, and explores religious attitudes to the purpose and importance of work.

Religion and the multicultural society

This topic explores the advantages and disadvantages of living in a multicultural society and considers the concepts of tolerance, respect and diversity.

Religion and identity

This topic considers what it means to be human, the physical and spiritual dimensions of life, and questions concerning image, views of 'self' and self-worth.

Religion and human rights

This topic looks at religious attitudes towards the law and human rights, and the impact of religion on the rights and responsibilities of the individual as a citizen.

■ Assessment guidance

The questions set in the examination will allow you to refer in your answers to the religion(s) you have studied. To encourage you to practise the type of question that will be set in the examination, each chapter has an assessment guidance section at the end. Each question in the examination will include an evaluation question that will be marked (out of six) by the examiner. It will help you to write better answers yourself if you understand what the examiners are looking for when they mark these questions. To assist you in this, you will be asked to mark an example answer yourself, using the mark scheme on page 7. Make sure that you understand the differences between the standard of answer for each level, and what you need to do to achieve full marks.

Examination questions will test two assessment objectives:

AO1	Describe, explain and analyse, using knowledge and understanding.	50%
AO2	Use evidence and reasoned argument to express and evaluate personal responses, informed insights, and differing viewpoints.	50%

The examiner will also take into account the quality of your written communication – how clearly you express yourself and how well you communicate your meaning. The grid opposite also gives you some guidance on the sort of quality examiners expect to see at different levels.

Introduction

Levels of response mark scheme for six-mark evaluation questions

Levels	Criteria for AO1	Criteria for AO2	Quality of written communication	Marks
0	Nothing relevant or worthy of credit	An unsupported opinion or no relevant evaluation	The candidate's presentation, spelling, punctuation and grammar seriously obstruct understanding	0 marks
Level 1	Something relevant or worthy of credit	An opinion supported by simple reason	The candidate presents some relevant information in a simple form. The text produced is usually legible. Spelling, punctuation and grammar allow meaning to be derived, although errors are sometimes obstructive	1 mark
Level 2	Elementary knowledge and understanding, e.g. two simple points	An opinion supported by one developed reason or two simple reasons		2 marks
Level 3	Sound knowledge and understanding	An opinion supported by one well developed reason or several simple reasons. **N.B. Candidates who make no religious comment should not achieve more than Level 3**	The candidate presents relevant information in a way which assists with the communication of meaning. The text produced is legible. Spelling, punctuation and grammar are sufficiently accurate not to obscure meaning	3 marks
Level 4	A clear knowledge and understanding with some development	An opinion supported by two developed reasons with reference to religion		4 marks
Level 5	A detailed answer with some analysis, as appropriate	Evidence of reasoned consideration of two different points of view, showing informed insights and knowledge and understanding of religion	The candidate presents relevant information coherently, employing structure and style to render meaning clear. The text produced is legible. Spelling, punctuation and grammar are sufficiently accurate to render meaning clear	5 marks
Level 6	A full and coherent answer showing good analysis, as appropriate	A well-argued response, with evidence of reasoned consideration of two different points of view showing informed insights and ability to apply knowledge and understanding of religion effectively		6 marks

Note: In evaluation answers to questions worth only 3 marks, the first three levels apply. These questions will themselves include a reference to a religion or a religious element, so candidates need to concentrate on giving their views and developing them. Questions that are marked out of 3 marks do not ask for two views, but simply for your opinion.

Successful study of this unit will result in a Short Course GCSE award. Study of one further unit will provide a Full Course GCSE award. Other units in Specification B which may be taken to achieve a Full Course GCSE award are:

Unit 2 Religion and Life Issues

Unit 3 Religion and Morality

Unit 4 Religious Philosophy and Ultimate Questions

Unit 5 Religious Expression in Society

Unit 6 Worship and Key Beliefs

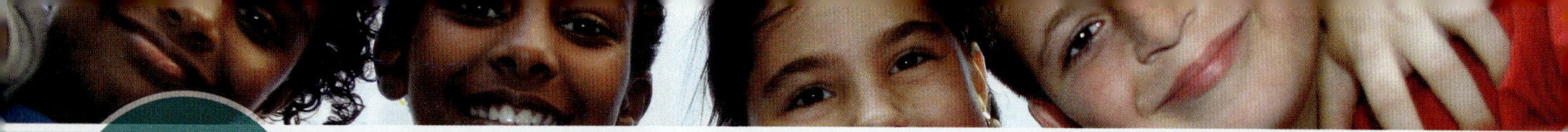

1 Religion and relationships

1.1 Relationships

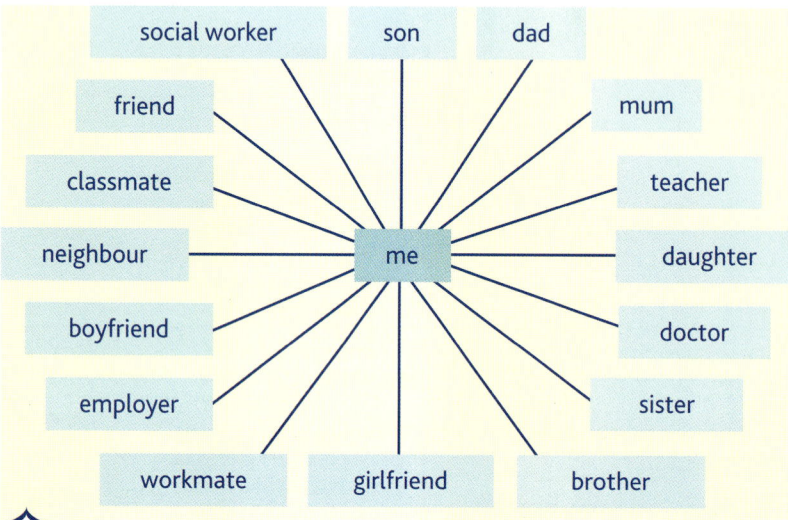

A *A relationships web*

Relationships connect us to other people. Any person could be one of the following to someone else: a mum or dad, a son or daughter, a sister or brother, a neighbour or friend, a boyfriend or girlfriend, a classmate or teacher, a doctor or social worker, an employer or workmate.

Learning about relationships

Most children first learn about relationships while growing up in a family. Babies learn to smile, talk and give and receive love in response to their parents. If a child has not had a good experience of family life when young, it often affects their relationships in school and in later life. After their families, children learn how to relate to others when they play with other children and have to share, take turns, be fair and play by the rules. In school they have to learn to get along with people from different backgrounds, cultures, religions and opinions. Friendship teaches young people the value of loyalty and trust, the enjoyment of sharing experiences, learning from each other, and making sense of the world. Good relationships lead to a happy and fulfilled life. Religions place emphasis on relationships, because through them people learn how to live responsibly in a community. It is also through human relationships that religious believers say people grow in their relationship with God.

Objectives

Think about the different relationships that connect us to other people.

Understand ideas about commitment, responsibility, contract and covenant.

Activities

1. Make a diagram of your own network of relationships. Use colour, or other means, to show the relationships that are most important to you, as compared with less important ones.

2. Is there such a thing as a perfect relationship? Explain your opinion.

Key terms

Marriage: a legal union between a man and a woman.
Commitment: a promise to be faithful.
Vows: promises made by the couple to be faithful to each other.
Contract: a formal agreement or legal bond.
Marriage contract: a contract between a bride and groom.
Covenant: an agreement.
Responsibility: the legal or moral duty which a person has.

B *We learn from our friends*

Key ideas

As young people mature physically their relationships mature too. This chapter is going to explore sexual relationships, **marriage** and the family in the context of religious beliefs. Here are some key ideas that underpin religious attitudes to these issues.

Commitment in marriage means making promises (**vows**) to be faithful to one's partner for life. Christians, Hindus and some Buddhists take vows at their wedding ceremonies.

A **contract** is a formal agreement and a **marriage contract** is a legal bond between the bride and groom. Hindus and Muslims regard the marriage ceremony itself as the legal and binding contract between the husband and wife. Jews have a contract that sets out the husband's responsibilities to his wife.

A **covenant** is a binding, lifelong agreement before God. Many Christians say God is a witness and partner to the promises a couple make to each other when they marry.

Responsibility means being accountable for one's own actions, and doing one's duty. In marriage, couples take on equal responsibility to love and care for each other and their children. Different religions and cultures divide the responsibilities in different ways. Jews and Muslims particularly value the mother's role in bringing up children in the faith.

Activities

3 What qualities do you think are most important in a friend?

4 What qualities do you think are most important in a boyfriend or girlfriend?

5 Are these the same? Give your reasons.

AQA Examiner's tip

Make sure you are able to explain the meaning of the key terms in relation to a religious understanding of sexual relationships.

Case study

The covenant

Covenant means a solemn oath, contract or bond. In the Bible, God made an everlasting covenant with Abraham and his descendants. God promised to make Abraham the father of a great people, to guide and protect his descendants and give them the land of Israel. In return, they had to obey God's laws (Genesis 12–17). Later, God renewed the covenant with Moses. If the people followed the Ten Commandments, God would make them his chosen people (Exodus 19–24).

Activity

6 Read the case study. Explain why the covenant of Abraham and Moses is a good symbol for a Christian marriage.

Summary

You should now be able to discuss how important it is to be able to form good relationships, and the importance religions place on them. You should be able to explain commitment, responsibility, contract and covenant in the context of marriage.

1.2 Sexual relationships

Human sexuality

Humans start to experience sexual feelings at puberty. This is a natural part of human biology that usually leads to intercourse with the opposite sex and reproduction (having children). A **heterosexual** relationship is a sexual relationship with a member of the opposite sex; that is, between a man and a woman. A **homosexual** (gay) relationship is a sexual relationship with a member of the same sex, either between a man and another man, or a woman and another woman.

Sexual relationships today

Attitudes towards sexual relationships have changed significantly over the last 60 years. Today there are more people who have:

- sex before marriage
- multiple sexual partners
- children outside marriage
- affairs (adultery)
- open homosexual relationships.

Sex is openly discussed in the media with the emphasis on sexual pleasure rather than on a deeply significant commitment between two people. Contraception and legal abortion have reduced the fear of pregnancy for unmarried people. Young single mothers are no longer forced to give up their babies for adoption, as many did in the past.

Homosexuality is now legal and gay couples can register their partnerships in civil ceremonies, which give them similar rights to married couples.

Despite sex education and the availability of contraception, the UK has the highest teenage pregnancy rate in Europe. The fact that teenagers seem to be having sex at a younger age is often raised as a matter for concern.

A *Attitudes to relationships have changed in recent years*

Objectives

Understand the meaning of heterosexual and homosexual relationships, and the age of consent.

Consider contemporary attitudes towards sexual relationships.

Key terms

Heterosexual: a human who is sexually attracted only to the members of the opposite sex.

Homosexual: a human who is sexually attracted only to members of the same sex.

Age of consent: the age at which someone can legally agree to have a sexual relationship.

links

Contraception and adultery are covered in more detail later in the book on pages 14 and 24.

Discussion activity

With a partner, in a group or as a whole class, decide which of the changes described are good, and which are not so good. Make notes on the opinions given, and the reasons for them.

Activities

1 Explain the difference between a heterosexual and a homosexual relationship.

2 Why do you think the UK has the highest teenage pregnancy rate in Europe? Explain your opinion.

The age of consent

The **age of consent** is the age at which someone can legally have a sexual relationship. In the UK, the age of consent for both boys and girls is 16 years. This applies to both heterosexual and homosexual relationships. The 2003 Sexual Offences Bill makes all sexual acts, not just intercourse, a criminal offence if at least one of the people involved, either male or female, is under 16 years old. The law is designed to protect children from exploitation or abuse by more powerful adults. Some people think this has criminalised young people who have under-age sex with others their own age.

> **Lowering the age of consent**
>
> People debate whether the age of consent should be lowered. They argue that some teenagers already have sex before the age of 16 and, as it is illegal, it is difficult to give them advice and support to prevent unwanted pregnancies, diseases and abuse. Opponents argue that a lower age of consent will encourage more young people to have sex earlier, with all the risks mentioned. A 1999 opinion poll showed that the majority of young people did not want the age of consent lowered or removed.

Case study

Across the world, the age of consent varies widely. These variations are often accepted because of religious or cultural differences, but some people think that it is wrong to allow too young an age of consent because children could be forced into sex and abused.

Activity

3 Should the age of consent be different for girls and boys, or for heterosexual and homosexual relationships? Explain your opinion.

Research activity

Use the internet or go to a library to find out how and when the age of consent in the UK came to be 16 years for boys and girls, heterosexuals and homosexuals alike.

Summary

You should now understand that sexuality is part of being human and be able to explain how attitudes towards heterosexual and homosexual relationships have changed over the last 60 years.

AQA Examiner's tip

'Explain your opinion' requires you to give reasons for your views. No marks are given for your opinion but, without it, the examiner will not know whether you have supported it with reasoned arguments.

1.3 Sex before marriage

Religious attitudes

When considering religious attitudes it is helpful to distinguish between **sex before marriage** (sex between two single people) and **sex outside marriage** or adultery (sex between two people where at least one of them is married).

In the past, sex before marriage was considered shocking, particularly for a girl. This is still true in Arab and Asian cultures, in which an unmarried girl who has sex may be asked to leave her home for bringing disgrace to her family.

No religion is in favour of sex before marriage, but some religious people might make a distinction between casual sex with different partners and sex with one partner in a committed relationship. However, all religions believe the proper place for sex is within marriage.

Buddhism

Buddhists think sex before marriage is harmful because it is based on a desire for pleasure, rather than **love**. Indulging in sex before marriage might encourage 'attachment' and 'craving' for sex that would result in suffering. The Third Precept forbids selfish or irresponsible sexual relationships that hurt or exploit others. A Buddhist should not pretend to love someone, nor persuade him or her to have sex before marriage.

Christianity

Christians believe sex expresses a deep, loving, lifelong union that requires the commitment of marriage. It is important to be sexually pure (chaste) before marriage. Christians believe it is wrong to use people as sex objects, and irresponsible to spread sexually transmitted infections or risk pregnancy. In the Bible St Paul urged sexual restraint and control (1 Corinthians 6:18–19).

A One Christian response has been the 'True Love Waits' campaign in which young people pledge not to have sex before marriage

Objectives

Understand religious attitudes to sex before marriage.

Links

Religious attitudes to sex outside marriage or adultery will be considered on page 24.

AQA Examiner's tip

Although sex before marriage is technically outside marriage, the specification makes a distinction between the terms. Later, you may be asked to think about whether there is a moral difference between sex before marriage and sex outside marriage.

Activity

1. Explain the difference between sex before marriage and sex outside marriage (adultery).

Key terms

Sex before marriage: sex between two single people.

Sex outside marriage: sex between two people where at least one of them is married.

Love: a feeling of deep affection, and in this case sexual attraction for someone.

Although the Church of England and the Roman Catholic Church officially teach that unmarried people should not have sex, some Christians accept that for some people sex before marriage is an expression of their love for each other.

Hinduism

Neither boys nor girls should have sex at the 'student stage', which comes before the 'householder stage', when Hindus are expected to marry and have a family.

Sensual pleasure, one of the four aims of a healthy and fulfilled life, should be fulfilled within marriage. Sex before marriage can damage a person's spiritual development. Many religious stories warn people about the problems created by unrestricted sexual activities.

Islam

Muslims see sex, a sacred gift of Allah, as an act of worship that contributes to Allah's creation. It is a strong instinct that must be controlled and enjoyed responsibly within marriage, not before. Muslims should dress modestly (Qur'an 24:30–31) and avoid leading others into sexual temptation. Sex before marriage (fornication) is expressly forbidden in the Qur'an and in some Muslim communities it is punishable by flogging (Qur'an 24:2–5).

Judaism

Sex is seen as a wonderful creation of God, not just for having children but also for giving pleasure and expressing a couple's love for each other throughout their marriage.

Sex before marriage is expressly forbidden in Judaism, and is thought to cheapen sex and lower a person's self-respect.

Sikhism

Sex before marriage is expressly forbidden. Family honour is important and girls, especially, must be modest. The Guru Granth Sahib teaches Sikhs to avoid anything that might lead to lust, one of the five evil passions. Sikhs avoid dancing or mixing with the opposite sex without a chaperone so that they are not tempted to be impure.

Activity

2 With a partner, in a group or as a class, make a list of the problems that might be created if there were no rules about sex. Share your ideas.

B *Muslim girls dress modestly*

AQA Examiner's tip

Make sure you are able to explain the attitudes of at least one religion towards sex before marriage.

Activity

3 'All sex before marriage is wrong.' Do you agree? Give reasons for your answer, showing that you have thought about more than one point of view. Refer to religious arguments in your answer.

Summary

You should now have a clear understanding that all religions teach that sex before marriage is wrong, and be able to explain the reasons for their views.

1.4 Religious attitudes to contraception

■ What is contraception?

Contraception is a way of preventing pregnancy when a couple have sex. The way different methods work influences religious attitudes about whether they are right or wrong.

Artificial methods

- The pill stops the woman from producing an egg.
- The diaphragm (cap) and condom stop the sperm meeting the egg. The condom also prevents the spread of sexually transmitted infections.
- The coil (intrauterine device) and the 'morning after' pill stop the fertilised egg from implanting in the womb. Some people consider these methods a form of abortion.
- Spermicidal jellies or creams kill the sperm directly.

Natural (rhythm) method

The couple avoids having sex during the woman's most fertile time each month. The woman works out when this is from changes in her body temperature.

Permanent method

Sterilisation (a surgical operation) of either the man or the woman is a permanent way of preventing pregnancy.

Buddhism

Buddhists accept most kinds of contraception if they are not used for selfish reasons. Rebirth takes place at conception (when the egg is fertilised by the sperm), so methods that cause an abortion are unacceptable to Buddhists who believe that no living beings should be harmed.

Christianity

The Roman Catholic and Orthodox Churches teach that artificial contraception goes against natural law. God's purpose for marriage is to have a family. Using contraception could encourage selfishness or infidelity. Parents should use the rhythm method to space the births of their children. Many Catholics disagree. The population explosion and spread of AIDS present new challenges to this teaching.

Other Christians allow contraception. Anglicans accept that people should only have as many children as they can reasonably afford. Bringing a baby into a life of deprivation would be unfair. Methodists allow contraception to enable couples to develop their relationship before having children, or to space pregnancies to avoid harming the mother's health.

Objectives

Understand religious attitudes to family planning and the use of contraception within marriage.

Key terms

Contraception: the artificial and chemical methods used to prevent pregnancy taking place.

AQA Examiner's tip

Although it is unlikely that you will be asked to describe different forms of contraception in the exam, it is important to know why religious people oppose or accept certain forms of contraception.

We believe in God.
We believe that sex is sacred.
We believe in caring for each other.
We believe in using condoms.

CATHOLICS FOR CHOICE | People of Faith Use Condoms
www.condoms4life.org | CATHOLICS FOR CHOICE

A An advert for the Condoms4Life campaign, which is a project of Catholics for Choice

Hinduism

A Hindu's duty is to marry and have children, particularly a son, required to perform important religious rituals. However, in India contraception is encouraged to reduce family size and poverty. Every human life is precious, so Hindus would not bring a child into the world to suffer. Couples can use any method of contraception as long as they practise non-harming.

Islam

Some Muslims oppose contraception because they believe Allah will give couples the strength to cope with any number of children. Most Muslims accept its use if both partners agree and do not use contraception to prevent having children altogether. Muslims accept contraception if a wife's health is at risk, in order to space pregnancies, to avoid passing on genetic disorders or because of serious financial difficulty. Muslims oppose methods that cause an abortion. They only accept sterilisation if a mother's life is at risk.

Judaism

A large family is a blessing from God. Jewish men are expected to father at least one son and one daughter. However, Reform and Progressive Jews accept contraception for many reasons, including social or financial reasons. The couple is free to choose their preferred method of contraception.

Orthodox Jews only allow contraception to prevent risk to the mother's health, to space out children or limit their number, but not to prevent having children altogether. The use of the pill is preferred by Orthodox Jews as it does not interfere with the sexual act (as does the rhythm method), or destroy semen (as do condoms). Sterilisation is forbidden because it damages the body God created.

Sikhism

Sikh sacred books give no specific guidance, so couples can decide whether to use contraception for the sake of the mother's health or welfare of their other children. Couples choose their own method, but sterilisation would only be used if medically necessary.

Beliefs and teachings

Buddhism 'Do not harm living beings'
the First Precept

and 'Right Intention'
the Buddhist Eightfold Path

influence Buddhist views.

Christianity (Roman Catholicism) Every sexual act should have the possibility of creating new life.
Humanae Vitae, 1968

Hinduism At the householder stage, a Hindu's 'dharma' is to marry and have children.

Islam Children are a gift from Allah, but contraception is accepted for good reasons by most Muslims, as long as both partners agree.

Judaism A woman may use contraception if a pregnancy would cause harm, if the woman is underage, already pregnant, or breast-feeding.
'The Beraita of the Three Women', from the Talmud

Sikhism There is no specific teaching on contraception. It is up to the couple to decide.

Activities

1. Why are some religious people against using the morning after pill?
2. 'Using artificial contraception encourages partners to be unfaithful.' What do you think? Explain your opinion.
3. 'Religions should not have a say about family planning.' Do you agree? Give reasons for your answer, showing that you have thought about more than one point of view.

AQA Examiner's tip

Remember that religions do not approve of sex before or outside marriage, so when they talk about contraception they are talking about its use by a married couple.

Summary

You should now be able to discuss the various religions' attitudes to artificial contraception, whether they accept it and the reservations they may have about the methods used.

1.5 The purpose and character of marriage

■ Why do people get married?

People get married to share their lives with the person they love. Marriage brings security because it is a serious, lifelong and public commitment. It is a legal contract that protects the rights of each partner and makes children born within marriage 'legitimate'. Marriage also has some financial advantages.

■ The purpose of marriage

Religions consider the desire for sexual intimacy and children natural. Therefore, marriage is the proper place to express sexuality, develop companionship and provide a secure environment to bring up children in a religious faith. As each partner develops qualities of love, trust, faithfulness and mutual consideration, marriage provides the means to grow spiritually and personally.

Objectives

Consider religious understandings of the purpose and character of marriage.

Extension activity

Make up your own list of vows or promises that you think a couple should be prepared to make to each other when they marry.

A Marriage is a legal contract

■ The character of marriage

Buddhism

Buddhists grow spiritually in marriage by practising loving kindness, compassion, faithfulness and respect. The ideal marriage is reflected in

links

The terms love, contract, commitment, responsibility and covenant are defined on pages 8 and 12, or you can look them up in the Glossary at the back of this book.

the responsibilities set out in scriptures. The man must show his wife respect, courtesy, appreciation and faithfulness and share authority with her in family matters. The wife must be faithful, hospitable to his family and friends, and skilful and conscientious in managing the household.

Christianity

Marriage is God's gift at the creation and a spiritual bond of trust. Christians believe marriage is a sacrament that reflects the sacrificial love of Jesus, and a covenant before God in which the couple promises to live faithfully together until death. The couple's physical intimacy expresses their love. They share companionship through good times and bad, and bring up children according to God's will.

Hinduism

Marriage is a religious duty at the householder stage that produces good 'karma'. Hindu marriage is a sacrament, blessed by God, and is the proper source of sexual pleasure, companionship and children. The man must be faithful to his wife, work hard to support his family, and perform the required rituals at their parents' deaths. The wife is responsible for 'puja' in the home, keeping house and bringing up children well. Rama and Sita provide role models for a good marriage.

Islam

Muslims are expected to marry. Marriage is a legal contract giving husband and wife equal rights under Allah. Since many marriages are arranged, Muslims believe that love will develop within the marriage, not necessarily before it. The ideal marriage should reflect mercy, love, peace, faithfulness and cooperation. The Qur'an teaches that husbands and wives should care for each other: they are like garments for each other (Qur'an 2:187).

Judaism

Marriage is part of God's plan at the creation. Jews have a duty to pass on their traditions to the next generation. Marriage is a lifelong commitment before God, like the love of God for his people Israel (shown in the covenant). It is also a contract (ketubah) in which the woman's financial security is protected. Traditionally, the man provides for his family and carries out religious obligations. The woman should obey her husband, manage the home and be a good mother. The ideal marriage is one where each partner's qualities complement each other to make a complete whole.

Sikhism

Sikhs have a duty to marry, as it is the way God intended men and women to live. Marriage is not just a legal contract. It is a union witnessed by God, a sacrament, a spiritual opportunity to become one spirit within two bodies. The ideal marriage reflects faithfulness, love, loyalty and happiness. The husband should gently guide and support his wife, and she should respect her husband and share the joys and sorrows of life with him as his equal.

Activities

1. Why do you think fewer people are getting married and more are having children without being married?

2. Why do people get married when so many couples divorce?

3. How might changing patterns of work affect the duties religions place on married people?

Research activity

Find out why Rama and Sita provide a role model for an ideal Hindu marriage.

AQA Examiner's tip

You need to be able to explain at least one religion's ideas about the purpose of marriage (what marriage is for) and the character of marriage (what marriage should be like) for the examination.

Summary

You should now be able to explain religious views on the purpose and character of marriage.

1.6 Religious weddings

■ Marriage ceremonies

Most religions mark the importance of marriage with a religious ceremony.

Buddhism

Buddhists have no formal religious ceremony, so customs vary. At some services the man and woman each take three sips of saki (rice wine), then repeat this twice, each time with a larger glass, to show the growing unity of husband and wife. Vows can be based on the Eightfold Path or Five Precepts, and some couples recite their responsibilities from the Sigilovdda Sutta.

Christianity

At most Christian weddings the couple make promises (vows) before God that they will remain faithful to each other until death, whatever the circumstances. Rings are exchanged as a sign of unending love and fidelity with the words:

> With my body I honour you, all that I am I give to you, and all that I have I share with you.
>
> Common Worship Services and Prayers for the Church of England: Marriage, The Archbishop's Council, 2000

Roman Catholics and Anglicans often have a service of Holy Communion held as part of the marriage service.

Hinduism

Hindu weddings can take several days. The best time is chosen through horoscopes. Henna patterns on the bride's hands and feet show the new life ahead of her. A white cord is placed around the couple's shoulders. They vow to love, cherish and protect each other throughout life. The priest ties the end of the bride's sari to the groom's scarf to symbolise unity. He lights a sacred fire showing God's presence, and the couple take seven steps around it. At each step they pray for food, strength, wealth, happiness, children, good health and unity. The couple are showered with flower petals and rice, representing blessings.

Islam

Muslims have a simple ceremony where the couple (or bride's representatives) declare, in front of at least two witnesses, that they freely consent to the marriage. They sign the marriage contract and the groom gives the bride an agreed amount of money that belongs to her alone. Readings from the Qur'an and a short sermon urge the couple to live a life of piety, mutual love, kindness and social responsibility. They may make vows and exchange rings, and a large feast celebrates the union of the two families.

> **Objectives**
>
> Know and understand religious marriage ceremonies.
>
> Understand the symbolism and meaning of marriage ceremonies for believers.

A 'Let man and woman, united in marriage, constantly exert themselves, that [they may not be] disunited [and] may not violate their mutual fidelity.'
Laws of Manu 9:102

Judaism

At a Jewish wedding, the marriage contract (ketubah) is signed in the presence of four witnesses and the rabbi. The ceremony (kidushin, meaning sanctification) is carried out under a canopy (chuppah), a symbol of an open home. The rabbi blesses the goblet of wine that is shared by the couple and plain, gold rings are exchanged. The ketubah is read out. After the blessing, the groom stamps on a wineglass to symbolise both the challenges of marriage and the destruction of the Jerusalem Temple.

links

The terms sacrament, covenant, commitment, contract, vows and responsibilities are defined on pages 8 and 18, or you can look them up in the Glossary at the back of this book.

B *'A man without a wife lives without joy, without blessing and without good.'*
Talmud

Sikhism

Sikh weddings must be held before the Guru Granth Sahib, the Sikh scripture. The couple is reminded of the purpose of marriage. Bowing to the Guru Granth Sahib shows that bride and groom accept its teachings and are committed to one another. The bride's father puts flower garlands over the couple and places one end of the groom's scarf in his daughter's hand, showing she is leaving her father to join her husband. The Lavan, a hymn that compares marriage to the soul's relationship with God, is sung. At the end of each verse, the couple circle the Guru Granth Sahib and bow to show they accept the Lavan's teachings. After karah parshad and a simple meal in the langar, the couple go to their new home.

AQA Examiner's tip

Make sure you are able to explain how one religion or Christian denomination celebrates marriage, and how the celebration reflects their understanding of marriage.

Activities

1. In the past, most people were married in a religious ceremony. In 2005, 66% of weddings took place in a registry office. Why do you think this is?

2. 'A religious wedding makes a couple's marriage stronger.' What do you think? Explain your opinion.

Summary

You should now be able to describe religious marriage ceremonies and explain their symbolism and meaning for believers.

1.7 Choices

■ Choosing a marriage partner

Choosing a marriage partner is one of the most important decisions someone can make. In some cultures young people choose for themselves; in others, parents arrange the marriage. Customs vary within religions and cultures.

Love

The romantic idea of falling in love, getting married and living happily ever after may work for some, but the divorce rate suggests that being 'swept off your feet' may not always be so reliable for a lifelong commitment.

All religions think love is essential for marriage. Those who have arranged marriages emphasise shared values and beliefs, and think that love develops after people marry, not necessarily before.

Parents

Most children hope their parents will like their future husband or wife. Most parents want their children to marry someone who will love, support and care for them, be good parents themselves and, for religious parents, share or at least respect their children's religion.

Some religious parents arrange or assist their children's marriage by looking for someone whose personality will suit their son or daughter, or who comes from a family they know. They look for someone of good character, background and education, who is healthy, has good job prospects and shares the same religion. Marriage is seen as uniting two families, rather than just the individuals involved. An arranged marriage is not a forced marriage, however. The man and woman both have a right to say 'no'.

Religion

Religions prefer people to marry a partner who will bring up children in their faith. Roman Catholics must marry in the Roman Catholic Church and a non-Catholic partner must allow the children to be brought up as Catholics. A Muslim woman must marry a Muslim; Muslim men can marry a Muslim, Christian or Jew. Orthodox Jews must marry from within their faith. Sikh women are expected to marry a Sikh. Arranged marriages are always with someone of the same religion.

Objectives

Consider religious responses to the issues of love, parental involvement and race in the choice of a marriage partner.

Understand alternatives to marriage, including celibacy, vocation to religious life, living together.

∞ links

The terms marriage, love and commitment are defined on pages 8 and 12, or you can look them up in the Glossary at the back of this book.

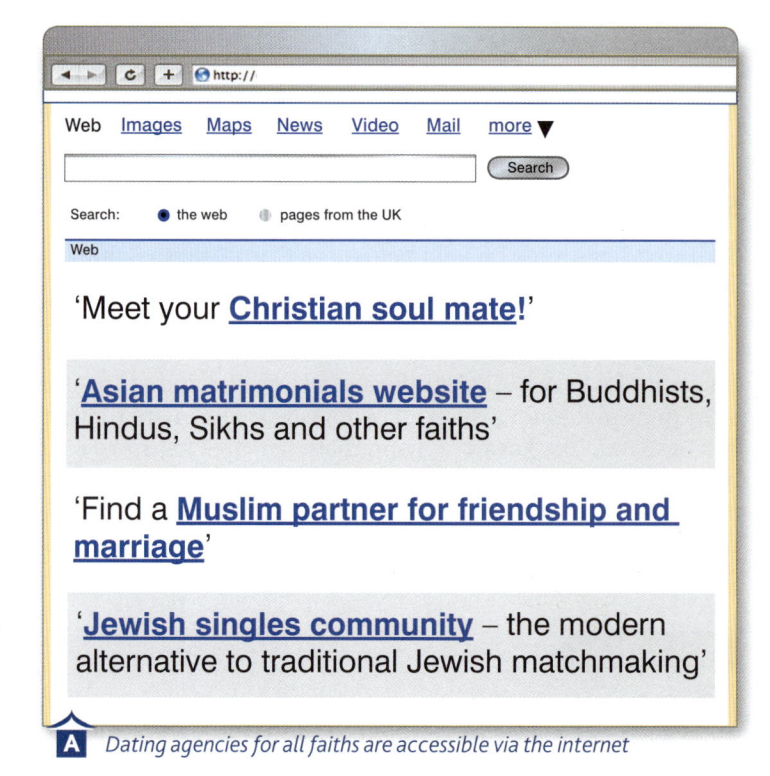

'Meet your **Christian soul mate**!'

'**Asian matrimonials website** – for Buddhists, Hindus, Sikhs and other faiths'

'Find a **Muslim partner for friendship and marriage**'

'**Jewish singles community** – the modern alternative to traditional Jewish matchmaking'

A Dating agencies for all faiths are accessible via the internet

Race

No religion stops mixed-race marriages. Everyone is equal and should be shown tolerance and respect. Buddhists, Christians, Muslims and Sikhs fully accept mixed race marriages. For Hindus, social class is more important than race. Jews are expected to marry Jewish partners so the children are considered Jewish, but race is not a problem.

Alternatives to marriage

Living together

Some couples live together before marriage to see if their relationship is going to work, but they often decide to marry if they are starting a family. Others never marry, but live together and raise their children as if they were married.

Civil partnerships

Civil partnerships are an alternative to marriage for homosexual couples wishing to have the same legal rights as married couples.

B *Religions accept mixed race marriages*

Celibacy

Some people choose to remain unmarried (celibate) and not to have sexual relationships. This may be for personal reasons, or as a way of showing their devotion to God.

Vocation to religious life

Some religious people are called to a religious way of life that requires celibacy. Roman Catholic priests, monks and nuns take vows of chastity (sexual purity or abstinence) and they do not marry so they can focus all their energies on their religious work.

Buddhism values celibacy as the way to achieve freedom from the cycle of rebirth. Buddhist monks and nuns vow to be celibate in order to concentrate on their own enlightenment and on helping others to follow the Buddha's teachings.

Activities

1. How important is it to marry someone who has a similar background to yourself? Give reasons for your answer.

2. Make a chart with four columns. List the advantages and disadvantages of living together, and the advantages and disadvantages of getting married. Discuss your findings with another member of the class.

Discussion activity

In pairs, discuss one of the following statements. Try to cover different points of view, and make notes of your discussion. Present your ideas and notes to a pair that has chosen the other statement.

- 'Parents know their children well so they are the best ones to choose a partner for them.'
- 'Marrying people of a different faith leads to arguments.'

AQA Examiner's tip

Evaluation questions ask you to give reasons for your answer, showing that you have thought about more than one point of view. You need to show an understanding of the complexity of the issue and give reasons why not everyone agrees with your view.

Summary

You should now have a clear understanding of religious responses to love, parental involvement and race in the choice of a marriage partner and be able to describe some alternatives to marriage.

1.8 Being a good parent

■ Being a good parent

Good parents love, care for and raise their children to know right from wrong. They teach them how to relate well to others and be good citizens. Religious parents raise their children within their faith.

Obvious? Not to everyone. In recent years the poor **parenting** skills of some people have been highlighted in television programmes. Experts sort out the bad behaviour of young children whose parents give in to their tantrums. 'Boot camps' teach badly behaved teenagers hard lessons in how to relate to other people.

> **Objectives**
> Understand the concepts of 'parenting' and 'the family'.
> Understand the role and importance of parents and family in religious faiths.

> **Key terms**
> **Parenting**: acting as a parent.
> **Family (The)**: a group of people who are related by blood, marriage or adoption.

> **Activities**
> 1. Finish the sentence, 'A good parent is someone who…' with a list of the qualities you think a good parent should have.
> 2. How do people learn how to be good parents? Should parenting be taught in schools? Explain your answers.

> **Research activity**
> Using the internet or a library, find some advice for being a good parent (put 'good parenting' into a search engine, for example). Does the advice given match your own ideas of what a good parent should be? Discuss your findings.

■ Family life

Family life has changed but the **family** is still considered the best environment for bringing up children and keeping society stable. The basic unit of a mother, father and children (a 'nuclear family') is still most common in the West, but in the UK today 25 per cent of children now live in single parent families. There are more 'blended families' or 'stepfamilies', where divorced people with children marry new partners with children of their own. Same-sex couples may legally adopt children in the UK.

In the past, families were larger and included grandparents and other relatives (an extended family) often living together. For most non-Western cultures, the extended family unit is most common.

■ Religious perspectives

All religions hold the family as particularly important in the religious upbringing of children.

A *Good parenting involves spending time with your children*

Chapter 1 Religion and relationships 23

Beliefs and teachings

Buddhists meditate on 'mother love' to understand what pure love or true compassion is. Buddhists are urged to care for their parents when they get old. By doing this they can repay their parents for bringing them up, nourishing them and introducing them to the world.

Christians believe children are gifts from God. They follow the commandment in the *Bible*, 'Honour your father and your mother'

Exodus 20:12

and Paul's teaching that fathers should not exasperate their children but bring them up as God instructs.

Ephesians 6:4

Hindus have close-knit extended families. All members work for the good of all and share the care and upbringing of children. The family repays its debt to elderly relatives by supporting them in retirement and old age. Fulfilling their duty in this way brings spiritual merit.

For **Muslims** the extended family is the basis of Islamic society and part of Allah's plan. The family shapes the moral values and character of children. Muslims care for elderly parents with kindness and respect because these parents loved and cared for their own children while they were young.

Qur'an 17:23–24

In **Jewish** families, particularly the mother, pass down the faith to the next generation. Many festivals are celebrated in the home where religious practices (welcoming Shabbat, dietary laws) and values of charity and hospitality are learned. Jews honour their parents as commanded in the *Torah*, and care for them in old age.

Proverbs 23:22

For **Sikhs**, the family is where children should first become aware of God, learn moral values and how to live with other people. Sikhs have large, extended families. Everyone supports each other to live, work, raise children and develop spiritually to reach God. The elderly members are respected and cared for and often a 'head of family' is chosen, either a man or a woman, who makes decisions and guides family members.

links

For more on the value religions attach to marriage and family life, re-read pages 16–17.

B *Religions teach respect for older members of the family*

AQA Examiner's tip

Be sure you can explain the meaning of 'parenting' and can explain what 'the family' means in Britain today.

Summary

You should now be able to discuss the high value religions place on being a good parent and the important role played by the family in bringing up children in a religious faith.

1.9 Sex outside marriage

■ Adultery

Adultery is having a sexual relationship (an affair) with someone who is not your spouse. It is often a reason for divorce in Britain. All religions place a high value on faithfulness in marriage. They teach that adultery is wrong because:

- it is a betrayal of trust that can destroy a relationship
- it breaks the marriage promises (vows) or contract between the partners
- it involves secrecy and lies
- it can affect the children and cause pain to all involved.

Discussion activity

With a partner, in a small group or as a class, list the reasons why someone might commit adultery (have an affair). Discuss how adultery might affect the people involved.

■ Religious attitudes

Buddhism

The Buddha taught that a married man should look upon other women as his mother, sister or daughter; he should not have sex with anyone but his wife. Adultery breaks the Third Precept – to avoid sexual misconduct. It is irresponsible, selfish and often results in unhappiness. A man who commits adultery lowers himself, his pleasure is restless and he is blameworthy (Dhammapada 309).

Christianity

Adultery destroys trust and breaks the promises (vows) Christian couples make before God. It threatens the stable relationship needed for children's security. The Bible commandment 'You shall not commit adultery' (Exodus 20:14) is clear. Jesus taught that lust, which could lead to adultery, is also wrong (Matthew 5:27–8). Jesus forgave a woman who was caught in adultery, but condemned her sin (John 8:1–11). For Christians marriage is an unbreakable bond that demands total faithfulness. Sex is a sacrament, a sign of Christ's love for the Church. Sex outside marriage cannot be that sign.

Hinduism

Adultery goes against the purpose of marriage by undermining its unbreakable bond and the stability of family life. Being unfaithful badly affects a person's karma and attempts to attain moksha (release from the cycle of rebirth). Yet adultery is not automatically a reason for divorce. The Laws of Manu tell wives to respect and obey their husbands even if they are unfaithful.

Objectives

Explore religious attitudes to sex outside marriage (adultery).

AQA Examiner's tip

Although the term adultery is not in the AQA specification, it is a clear way of distinguishing between sex *before* and *outside* marriage.

links

The term 'adultery' is defined in the Glossary at the back of this book.

Research activity

Find out using the internet or a library about recent research on why people commit adultery. Are the reasons different for men and women? Can a marriage survive adultery by one of the partners?

Extension activity

Think about the way adultery is portrayed in television programmes or in newspaper stories. Do you think most people in Britain agree with religions that sex outside of marriage is wrong? Give reasons for your views, and give examples from the media that support your opinions.

Islam

Adultery is considered a serious sin in Islam and Muslims are urged to avoid anything that could open the way for improper sexual behaviour to take place. The Qur'an warns Muslims to have nothing to do with adultery as it is shameful and opens the way to other evils (Qur'an 17:32). The Qur'an says that a woman and man guilty of adultery or fornication should each be flogged with a hundred stripes (Qur'an 24:2).

Judaism

In the Torah the commandment 'You shall not commit adultery' (Exodus 20:14) only applies to sex between a married woman and a man who is not her husband. It is considered a most serious sin, and was punishable by the death of both the man and the woman. Today, there is no death penalty, but a woman who commits adultery becomes forbidden to both her husband and her lover. She must be divorced.

Sikhism

Sikhs must be faithful in marriage. Adultery betrays trust and brings shame on the family. It is one of four misdeeds (kurahat) that members of the Khalsa must not commit. Lust is one of five evil passions. The Kachera (underwear worn by men and women, one of the Five Ks) reminds Sikhs that they must be faithful and sexually pure in marriage. A Sikh should respect another man's wife as he would his own mother and avoid looking lustfully at someone else's wife (Guru Granth Sahib 274).

Activity

1. Answer the following questions, giving reasons for your opinions. Try to include religious arguments for or against the quotation.
   a. 'Sex before marriage is not as bad as sex outside marriage.' What do you think?
   b. 'Adultery is the ultimate crime against the family.' Do you agree?

A Adultery can cause much unhappiness

AQA Examiner's tip

You need to be able to explain the attitudes of at least one religion towards sex outside marriage (adultery) for your examination.

Summary

You should now have a clear understanding that all religions teach that sex outside marriage is wrong, and be able to explain the reasons why.

1.10 Divorce

Divorce in Britain

'Advice about **finances after divorce**'
'**Divorce counselling** and help'
'Complete **DIY divorce solution** offered'
'Contact us for advice on **Divorce Law**'
'**Getting divorced?** – Look no further for your survival toolkit!'
'Let us help you find your **divorce solicitor**'

A *The internet offers much advice about divorce*

One third of all marriages in Britain end in divorce. Some religions have their own divorce courts, but couples in Britain must obtain a legally recognised civil divorce. Divorce is allowed after one year of marriage if the marriage cannot be saved. People can re-marry as many times as they wish.

Religious attitudes

All religions try to help couples that are having problems. Muslim families will act as mediators for the couple's reconciliation. Christian clergy offer couples counselling, prayer and the sacraments. Jewish couples may turn to the rabbi for advice. Religions differ about marrying someone else after divorce.

Buddhism

In Buddhist countries there is social pressure not to divorce, and Buddhists try to avoid selfishness and intolerance that can lead to unhappy marriages. They accept that for some unhappy couples, it is more compassionate to allow divorce to limit suffering, despite its harmful consequences, if Right Intention is present.

Christianity

In the Bible Jesus taught that anyone who divorced and re-married was committing adultery (Mark 10:2–12). The Church helps divorced people, but must also keep marriage sacred. Vows made in God's presence should be kept.

- Roman Catholics can separate but they cannot marry someone else while their partner is still alive. Catholics can obtain an annulment if it was never a true marriage.
- Divorced Anglicans can marry someone else in church with the bishop's permission, but this depends on the priest, as some think vows can only be made once. Some will offer a blessing after a civil ceremony.
- The Eastern Orthodox Church grants divorces and re-marries couples, but usually not more than twice.

> **Objectives**
> Know and understand religious attitudes to divorce and re-marriage.

> **Key terms**
> Divorce: the legal ending of a marriage.

> **AQA Examiner's tip**
> Be clear what you mean by re-marriage. Christian attitudes differ about re-marriage to a different partner after divorce, but most would not object to a couple re-marrying each other (renewing vows or having a blessing) after civil divorce.

- Protestant churches accept civil divorce and allow re-marriage in church as long as the couple take the vows seriously.

Hinduism

Hindu scriptures forbid a woman leaving her husband under any circumstances. Marriage is a sacred bond for life and the duty to raise a family comes before any difficulties the couple may have. Indian civil law (1955) allows divorce for cruelty, adultery, desertion or being unable to have children after fifteen years of marriage. Hindus rarely marry again because many feel divorce is shameful.

Islam

For Muslims, divorce is 'hateful to Allah' (Hadith) but is permitted as a last resort. The couple must wait three months to see if the wife is pregnant and to allow reconciliation if possible (Qur'an 4:35). A husband must return any dowry and support his wife until she re-marries. A wife can divorce her husband, but he does not have to support her if he is not at fault, and she must repay the marriage gift. He must still support his children in all cases.

B *Children suffer when their parents argue*

Judaism

Jewish couples can divorce if they no longer love each other 'as one flesh' and all attempts at reconciliation have failed. The Torah says a man can divorce his wife if 'he finds something indecent about her' (Deuteronomy 24:1). A civil divorce is not sufficient. The husband, with his wife's consent, must begin a religious divorce ('get') to break the marriage contract (ketubah). Jews regret divorce but encourage people to re-marry.

Sikhism

Sikhs reluctantly accept civil divorce. The couple's families will do everything they can to prevent the separation. The grounds for divorce include adultery, cruelty, desertion, insanity, change of religion and male impotence. Sikhs are encouraged to re-marry in the gurdwara.

Research activity

Using the internet or a library, find out more about the religious rules about divorce in the religion(s) you are studying.

Discussion activity

1. Divide into three groups, with each group discussing one of the following statements, considering different points of view. Each group should then report back to the class on their discussion.
   a. 'Divorce is far too easy.'
   b. 'Being a member of a religion is helpful to people whose marriages are in trouble.'
   c. 'Divorced people should not be allowed to re-marry in a religious ceremony.'

AQA Examiner's tip

You need to know the attitudes of at least one religion about divorce. Remember that opinions within a religion may also vary, so it is helpful to say 'most Christians' or 'some Hindus' when describing what religious people think.

Summary

You should now have a clear understanding that all religions teach that marriage is for life and be able to discuss the different attitudes of religions to the breakdown of marriage, divorce and re-marriage.

Assessment guidance

1

Religion and relationships – summary

For the examination you should now be able to:

- ✓ explain the concepts of commitment, responsibility, contract and covenant
- ✓ explain the difference between heterosexual and homosexual relationships and the law governing such relationships (the age of consent)
- ✓ outline religious attitudes towards sexual relationships before and outside marriage
- ✓ explain religious understandings of the purpose and character of marriage
- ✓ outline religious marriage ceremonies and the concepts of contracts and vows
- ✓ discuss alternatives to marriage and religious responses to the issues involved in the choice of a marriage partner
- ✓ explain the concepts and role of parenting and the family from a religious perspective
- ✓ explain religious attitudes towards contraception and divorce
- ✓ apply sacred texts, religious principles and/or statements by religious authorities to these issues.

AQA Examiner's tip: Try to use key terms like 'commitment', 'responsibility', 'contract' and 'covenant' in your answer. This shows a higher level of skill to the examiner.

Sample answer

1 Write an answer to the following examination question:

'Couples who are having problems should stay together for the sake of their children.'*

Do you agree? Give reasons for your answer, showing that you have thought about more than one point of view. Refer to religious arguments in your answer.

(6 marks)

(*Source: AQA B1 examination question 2007)

2 Read the following sample answer.

> I do not agree because it is upsetting for children to hear their parents fight. If one partner is abusive, they should separate. Muslims allow divorce if the couple cannot resolve their difficulties with the help of both families.
>
> However, Christians make vows before God that they will be faithful and stay together until death. Jesus taught forgiveness of each other's faults. But I think it depends on how bad the problems are that the couple are having.

3 With a partner, discuss the sample answer. Do you think that there are other things that the student could have included in the answer?

4 What mark (out of 6) would you give this answer? (Look at the mark scheme in the Introduction on page 7 (AO2) before you attempt this.) What are the reasons for the mark you have given?

AQA Examination-style questions

1 Look at the photograph and answer the following questions.

    (a) Give **two** responsibilities that couples accept when they marry. *(2 marks)*

    (b) Explain the ways in which religious belief might influence the choice of a marriage partner. *(4 marks)*

    (c) 'Couples should have religious weddings.' What do you think? Explain your opinion. *(3 marks)*

    (d) Explain briefly religious teachings about contraception within marriage. *(3 marks)*

    (e) 'The only purpose of marriage is to have children.' Do you agree? Give reasons for your answer, showing that you have thought about more than one point of view. Refer to religious arguments in your answer. *(6 marks)*

> **AQA Examiner's tip**
>
> Remember when you are asked if you agree with a statement, you must show what you think and the reasons why other people might take a different view. If your answer is one sided, you can only achieve a maximum of 4 marks. If you make no comment about religious belief or practice, you will achieve no more than 3 marks.

2 Religion, sport and leisure

2.1 Stress and relaxation

A Revising for exams can be stressful

Objectives
Examine the problem of stress and the need for relaxation.

Consider different types of relaxation.

Stress

There are so many pressures that everyone faces in life that, from time to time, we all feel stressed. Some pressure can be beneficial if it inspires motivation and commitment, but too much pressure is not a good thing. **Stress** results from excessive pressure and this can lead to ill health. Those under stress may suffer from panic attacks, headaches, muscle tension, high blood pressure, sleeplessness, depression and fatigue.

Some of the signs of stress include:

- inability to concentrate or make decisions
- failure to delegate
- overworking
- behaviour changes, for example becoming tearful, withdrawn, irritable or aggressive
- loss of self-confidence
- increased smoking or drinking
- increased absence through sickness.

Key terms
Stress: the mental or physical distress caused by pressure or difficult circumstances.

Relaxation: the act of relaxing the body and/or mind in order to become less tense.

Stress relief: the reduction or removal of mental or physical distress.

Exercise: physical activity intended to improve strength and fitness.

Relaxation

> *What I dream of is an art of balance, of purity and serenity, devoid of troubling or depressing subject matter, ... a soothing, calming influence on the mind, something like a good armchair that provides relaxation from fatigue.*
>
> Henri Matisse

B Some may find a warm bath the ideal way to relax

The importance of relaxation

Relaxation is a form of **stress relief**. It helps to keep our stress levels down and as a consequence improves our health. Everybody needs to find the time to relax and there are many techniques that can be used to help do this, such as listening to soothing music, practising yoga, massage, or taking up a hobby. Regular relaxation reduces the risk of heart attacks, improves memory, helps the immune system and gives protection from mental health problems. It also gives the opportunity of spending time with family and friends. Many people also believe in balancing work and relaxation and having time to reflect and focus on spiritual things.

> ### Case study
>
> ### Meditation
>
> Buddhists have practised meditation for thousands of years as a method of getting in touch with deep feelings and of trying to free the mind of disturbing emotions, such as hatred, anger and jealousy. There are different forms of Buddhist meditation but they have the aim of helping the person to reach enlightenment. In modern times, thousands of people use meditation as a means of stress relief and improving health. Some find a quiet place and allow their overactive minds to become calm and more peaceful. Some focus on an object, such as a candle, a sound, their breathing or a flower. A deep state of relaxation and tranquillity follows as all other thoughts fade away.

C *Yoga may be used to reduce stress*

Extension activity

Use the internet or a library to find out about the use of yoga to improve health or fitness, and by Hindus as an aid to achieving 'moksha'.

Exercise

For many people, physical **exercise** is a form of relaxation. This may take the form of road running, swimming, or special relaxation exercises. Other people visit the gym regularly, play golf, walk or become involved in team sports. Exercise promotes fitness of the body and the mind.

Discussion activity

With a partner, in a small group or as a whole class discuss the following Chinese proverb:

'Tension is who you think you should be. Relaxation is who you are.'

Do you agree? Make notes on the opinions given, and the reasons for them.

links

Find out more about exercise on pages 32–33.

Activities

1. Explain why people become stressed.
2. What effect does stress have on a person?
3. Give three examples of ways in which a person may relax.
4. 'You can relax more by doing exercises than by meditating.' What do you think? Explain your opinion.

Summary

You should now be able to discuss the pressures of life and the importance of relaxation in helping to overcome stress.

AQA Examiner's tip

Make sure that you know:
- the effects and signs of stress
- why relaxation is important
- some relaxation techniques.

2.2 Leisure

Leisure

The **leisure** industry in Britain is vast. It provides leisure centres, sports halls, swimming pools, art galleries, theatres, museums and much more. Leisure opportunities vary from the very active, such as mountaineering, to the very passive, such as watching television. What might seem a leisure activity to one person, such as taking a long walk along a coastal path, might be considered hard work by someone who is not fit and does not share a love of the outdoors. What suits one person might be regarded as uninspiring by another.

> **Objectives**
> Investigate religious attitudes towards the purpose, use and importance of leisure.

> **Key terms**
> **Leisure**: free time. Time when an individual is not working.
> **Healthy living**: living a life which is good for the body, both physically and mentally.
> **Pilgrimage**: a physical journey to a special place. It can also be a person's inner spiritual journey.

A Climbing a mountain

The purpose and importance of leisure

Leisure is vitally important, as without it life would not be as interesting and worthwhile. Leisure activities are an essential part of **healthy living** and help to:

- prevent boredom
- refresh a person physically and mentally
- encourage social relationships and a feeling of belonging
- improve a person's enjoyment and satisfaction with life
- encourage the development of new skills and interests
- stimulate creativity and inventiveness.

Religious attitudes to leisure

All religions recognise the value and need for leisure time as a time for refreshment and renewing of the body, mind and spirit. In addition, it gives believers the opportunity to practise their faith, develop their spirituality and appreciate the beauty and wonder of creation. Observing a beautiful sunset, or dew on a cobweb, or the sky at night may have a profound effect on those who see it.

B Reading is a popular leisure activity

> **Beliefs and teachings**
> When I consider your heavens, the work of your fingers, the moon and the stars, which you have set in place, what is man that you are mindful of him, the son of man that you care for him?
> *Psalm* 8:3–4

Time can be spent in worship, prayer or meditation, in the home, place of worship or in a quiet location. The gospels tell how Jesus often left the crowds to spend time communicating with God. Buddhists remember how the Buddha spent time meditating in his search for enlightenment.

Leisure time enables believers to participate fully in the life of their faith community and receive teaching about their religion. In addition to worship on holy days, many young people take part in youth activities run by believers, including religious youth clubs, sports teams, summer camps and adventure holidays. Community service and voluntary work may also provide a focus for leisure time.

Pilgrimage to holy sites and shrines

Leisure time may give the opportunity to religious believers to go on a **pilgrimage**. For example, Buddhists may wish to go to Bodh Gaya to celebrate where the Buddha gained enlightenment. Millions of Hindus visit Varanasi (Benares) and the River Ganges, and Jews and Christians go to Israel to see the historical sites associated with their faith. Muslims take part in the once in a lifetime experience of the Hajj, and Sikhs may visit Amritsar and the Golden Temple.

links
Find out more about community service and voluntary work by reading page 66.

Examiner's tip
Make sure that you are able to explain the importance of leisure and how leisure may help a believer develop his or her spirituality.

Research activity
Use the internet or a library to find out more about the pilgrimage sites of your chosen religion(s).

The Parable of the Rich Fool (Luke 12:16–20)
In the Bible Jesus told of a rich man who grew an enormous crop of corn on his land. He decided to pull down his barns and build larger ones so that he could get every last grain stored. He worked extremely hard without any time for leisure, and when he had finished he said to himself that he could now take life easy by eating, drinking and enjoying himself. But God said that he was a fool because that night he would die and so would have no time to enjoy the riches he had earned.

Discussion activity
With a partner, in a group or as a whole class, discuss the following statement.

'Too many people use leisure time selfishly and miss the opportunity of developing their spirituality.'

Make notes on the opinions given.

Activities
Answer the following questions:

1. Explain why leisure activities may help a person.
2. Explain why leisure time is important to a religious believer.
3. What does the Parable of the Rich Fool (see above) teach about work and leisure?

Summary
You should now be able to discuss the importance of leisure and the opportunities its gives to help a believer strengthen his or her faith and be of benefit others.

2.3 Benefits of leisure

The positives of leisure

Leisure gives people the chance to take part in activities that may help to bring satisfaction mentally, socially, physically and spiritually. Leisure provides the opportunity to:

- relax the mind, for example by watching a movie, listening to music or reading a book
- stretch the mind, for example by learning another language or doing something creative
- socialise and meet new people, for example by dancing, joining a club or religious group
- obtain peace, for example by sitting quietly in the open air
- serve others and do voluntary work, such as helping to support a charity
- improve fitness by working out in the gym, or taking part in sport
- replenish energy after a hard day's work, for example by watching television or a taking up a hobby
- pursue spiritual activities, such as prayer or meditation.

Creativity

Leisure time gives people the opportunity to take part in **creative activities**, and to develop their talents. Some peoples' talents are used in worship. For example, dance may be used to interpret a sacred story. Muslim artists have created much admired geometric patterns which decorate mosques, such as the Dome of the Rock in Jerusalem. Musicians and song writers have received the **inspiration** to write songs, musicals and oratorios which reflect their faith. Graham Kendrick's modern worship songs, Handel's *Messiah* and Lloyd Webber's *Joseph and his Technicoloured Dreamcoat* are all examples of this creativity.

> **Objective**
> Investigate the positive value of leisure.

> **Key terms**
> **Creative activities**: activities that involve imagination and original thought, often in making things.
> **Inspiration**: the stimulation of the mind that leads a person to do something creative.
> **Natural ability**: an ability that is inherited and which is revealed by a quickness to learn, understand or acquire a skill.

A Muslims are inspired to decorate their mosques beautifully

Case study

The Hindi language film industry in India has been given the informal name 'Bollywood'. Indian cinema has been built on the dramatisation of the great Hindu epics of the Ramayana and Mahabharata. Production is prolific and the films are mostly musicals. Religious belief is found in nearly every theme because at the heart of most films is the struggle between good and evil. A story with a moral is essential, and many plots include a Hindu boy falling in love with a Muslim girl. It is rare for anyone other than a Hindu to be the hero.

B Buddhist temple drums

> **Research activity**
> 1. Use the internet, or a library, to find out about how religion inspired Michelangelo's work.

C Girls learning to dance

D Gospel singers

Music

Music is a vital part of the leisure industry. From seeing live bands to listening to CDs or iPods, music is a major ingredient in British culture. Music is also an important element of worship in Christianity, Hinduism, Judaism and Sikhism as it is used in praise and in proclaiming the beliefs of the faith.

Research activity

2. Use the internet, or a library, to find out about music used in worship in the religion(s) you are studying.

Natural ability and the source of skills

Many religious believers think that **natural ability** is a gift from God. For example, the hand-eye coordination that is needed to catch a ball, or the ability to create classical music or paint a masterpiece is thought of as a blessing from God. Practice improves that gift but the natural ability that a person has is regarded as God's gift. For example, Muslims believe that the source of all skills is Allah.

Activities

Answer the following questions:

1. Give examples of how leisure can help a person to be creative.
2. Explain what is meant by 'natural ability'.
3. Describe briefly how religious beliefs are included in Bollywood films.
4. Explain some of the benefits that may be derived from leisure time.

Discussion activity

With a partner, in a small group or as a class discuss the following statement.

'Being creative and worshipping God through music, art, dance or drama is the best way to use leisure time.'

What do you think? Make notes on the opinions given and the reasons for them.

AQA Examiner's tip

Make sure you are able to explain how leisure helps religious believers to live fulfilled lives.

Summary

You should now be able to explain how leisure may benefit a person socially, physically, mentally and spiritually.

2.4 Misuse of leisure

Objectives
Examine examples of how leisure may be misused.

A waste of leisure

During leisure time some people commit vandalism, immorality or take drugs in an attempt to find excitement. Others are involved in **gambling** or **binge drinking**. Gambling is a multi-million pound industry with bets being placed on almost anything, including the outcome of football matches and horse races in the hope of winning.

A Roulette

B Cards and chips at a casino

Gambling

Casinos

Casinos provide a variety of gambling opportunities with slot machines and games of chance. The odds are stacked against the players as the casino expects to make a profit. Other games, such as blackjack and poker, involve some skill but the casino takes a commission. Las Vegas, in the USA, attracts millions of customers to play in its casinos but the vast majority end up as losers.

Online casinos are booming and addiction to gambling is a growing problem.

> **Case study**
>
> **Gambling**
>
> Ed began playing slot machines on a school trip and got a taste for gambling. While at university he was introduced to casinos and became addicted. He borrowed from banks, family and friends – anywhere he could, as all he could think of was the turn of the next card. He dropped out of education, lost his job and his friends. The urge to gamble caused him to ignore the financial, physical or emotional consequences. He lost everything and ran up thousands of pounds of debt on credit cards.

Religious beliefs about gambling

Gambling appeals to selfishness and greed. Most people are losers, and winners benefit at the expense of others. Many become addicted and lose money, causing real hardship to themselves and their families. Religions oppose gambling.

Beliefs and teachings

Buddhism 'There are six evil results of gambling viz. loss of money, the winner is hated, the loser grieves over his losses, his word is unreliable, he is despised by friends and not fit to have a wife.'

'The Layman's Code of Discipline', from the Sigalovada Sutta

Christianity 'People who want to get rich fall into temptation and a trap and into many foolish and harmful desires that plunge men into ruin and destruction.'

1 Timothy 6:9

Hinduism 'Play not with dice: No, cultivate thy corn land. Enjoy the gain and deem that wealth sufficient.'

Rigved 10:34:13

Islam 'Believers, wine and games of chance, idols and divining arrows, are abominations devised by Satan.'

Qur'an 5:90

Judaism The Talmud classifies dice players (people who live off winnings from gambling) as invalid witnesses in a court of law.

Sikhism One of the duties of a Sikh is to avoid gambling, begging or working in the alcohol or tobacco industries.

Chapter 2   Religion, sport and leisure   37

C   Celebrating with a drink

D   40% of admissions to A & E are drink related

Key terms

Gambling: playing games of chance for money.

Binge drinking: consuming an excessive amount of alcohol in a short amount of time.

Casino: a place where people play games of chance, such as roulette, blackjack and poker.

Binge drinking

Binge drinking

Teenagers are drinking at an earlier age and more heavily than ever before. The annual cost to the economy of binge drinking is over 20 billion pounds, and alcohol-related problems cause the premature death of over 20,000 people per year. Hangovers, absenteeism from work, drink-related violence, crime and illness are major problems. A government report estimated that each year drinking causes 1.2 million incidents of violence and parents with drink problems affect 1.3 million children. Forty per cent of admissions to the accident and emergency services in the hospitals are related to alcohol.

Case study

Religious beliefs and teachings about drinking

Excessive drinking causes drunkenness, ill-treatment of children, marriage problems, loss of reasoning and moral integrity, and damages the body (God's temple). All religions condemn the excessive consumption of alcohol, and some forbid it altogether.

Beliefs and teachings

Buddhism 'I undertake to refrain from intoxicating drinks and drugs which lead to carelessness.'
Fifth Precept

Christianity 'Do not get drunk on wine, which leads to debauchery.'
Ephesians 5:18

Hinduism 'All those which produce molasses and such intoxicants are to be forbidden by those who desire spiritual rewards.'
Laws of Manu

Islam 'They ask you about drinking and gambling. Say: "There is great harm in both ...."'
Qur'an 2:219

Judaism 'Drinking too much makes you loud and foolish. It's stupid to get drunk.'
Proverbs 20:1

Sikhism 'By drinking wine one loses sanity and becomes mad, loses the power of discrimination and incurs the displeasure of God.'
Adi Granth 554

Discussion activity

With a partner, in a small group or as a class, discuss ways (other than gambling and binge drinking) that leisure time may be misused. Make notes on the ideas given.

Activities

Answer the following questions:

1. 'The only real winners of gambling are the owners of the casinos.' What do you think? Explain your opinion.

2. Re-read the case study about Ed and explain how he ruined his life.

3. Re-read the case study about binge drinking and explain why religious believers are opposed to drinking too much.

AQA Examiner's tip

Be prepared to explain the problems associated with gambling and binge drinking and religious belief about this misuse of leisure.

Summary

You should now be able to explain religious believers' concerns about gambling and binge drinking.

2.5 Religion and sport

Objectives
Know and understand the benefits of sport.

Investigate religious attitudes to sport.

What are the benefits of sport?

Participation in **sport** improves general health and wellbeing. Exercise helps a person have a healthy lifestyle as it assists the control of bodyweight and strengthens bones. Regular sports activity:

- improves concentration and stamina
- helps fight anxiety and depression
- improves physical skills, including coordination, flexibility and balance
- gives a sense of belonging and the opportunity to work as a team
- provides opportunities to socialise with people of similar interests.

Sport can inspire an individual to develop skills and improve their talent. **Teamwork** skills are developed, together with a sense of purpose and an appreciation of the value of working together to achieve a common goal.

Key terms
Sport: physical activity that is governed by a set of rules or customs; it is usually competitive.

Teamwork: working together for the benefit of the whole team.

Sabbath: a day of rest and worship.

Religious beliefs about sport

Most religious believers appreciate the value of sport providing it does not involve cheating and dishonesty.

Buddhism

An important part of Buddhist morality is based on right intention so if taking part in sport is to be of benefit then there is no problem. Actions performed out of ignorance, greed or hatred can be immoral. So sports such as boxing, where the aim is to disable your opponent, are generally not supported by Buddhists.

Christianity

Christians believe that sport is good so long as it does not become an idol or more important than the person's relationship with God. Sport keeps the God-given body healthy and enables people to work with one another.

Hinduism

One of the Hindu four aims of life is 'kama' or enjoyment. Hindus support sport as it brings pleasure and balance to life and games like cricket and hockey are well supported in India. Judo and Karate originated in the Hindu culture of India as well as other leisure activities such as chess, ludo, playing cards and polo.

Islam

Physical fitness is encouraged in Islam but concerns about modesty restrict the participation of women in some sports. Muhammad took part in wrestling, racing, archery and horse racing.

A *Martial arts such as Judo and Karate originated in the Hindu culture of India*

Beliefs and teachings
Teach your sons the art of swimming, sharp shooting and horseback riding.

Omar, the second Caliph

∞ links
Look at page 41 to see more detail about modesty, Muslim women and sport.

Judaism

During the time of the Greek and Roman Empires, Jews were not sports lovers. This is not the case today except among some ultra-orthodox Jews. Sport is big business in Israel with Jews participating particularly in water sports, football, basketball, tennis and athletics.

Sikhism

During the early days of Sikhism, followers were often under attack and the gurus introduced sports, which helped to strengthen their fighting abilities. This included competition in martial arts, horse riding, spear throwing, archery, sword fighting, wrestling and athletics. Nowadays, hockey and cricket are very popular among Sikhs.

B Water sports are popular in Israel

C Sikhs compete in horse racing and wrestling

Holy days

Some religious believers disagree with sport on festival days or the Sabbath. They argue that, for example, ball games and cycle rides are fine on weekdays but the Sabbath is a rest day, a day set apart for God. If sporting events avoided holy days it would prevent games from taking place on Fridays for Muslims, Saturdays for Jews and Sundays for Christians.

Activities

Write an answer to each of the following questions:

1. Explain the benefits of taking part in sport.
2. Explain religious attitudes towards sport in the religion(s) you have studied.
3. 'Sports should not take place on holy days.' Do you agree? Give reasons for your opinion.

Case study: 'The Flying Scotsman'

Committed Christian, Eric Liddell, often called the 'Flying Scotsman', was selected to run in the Paris Olympics 1924. His best event was the 100 metres, but the schedule meant that he would need to run on a Sunday (the Sabbath Day). Liddell was not prepared to break the commandment 'Remember the Sabbath Day by keeping it holy' (Exodus 20:8), so he withdrew from the 100 metres and ran the 400 metres instead, as it was not taking place on a Sunday. Remarkably, he won the race and broke the world record in the process.

Extension activity

Watch the film *Chariots of Fire* (the story of Eric Liddell) or the film *Bend it like Beckham* which highlights conflict in a Sikh family over a daughter who wishes to play football, and focus on the religious beliefs it shows about sport.

AQA Examiner's tip

Make sure that you know the attitudes of the religion(s) you have studied to taking part in sport.

Discussion activity

With a partner, in a small group or as a class, discuss whether you agree with former Prime Minister, Tony Blair, when he said, 'Investment in sport is not just a sports policy. It is a health policy, an education policy, an anti-crime policy and an anti-drugs policy.'* Make notes on the opinions given and the reasons for them.

*(Source: http://www.nottinghamcity.gov.uk/emsports/docs/storybook.pdf)

Summary

You should now be able to discuss how sport improves general health and wellbeing and give reasons why some believers do not think they should take part in sport played on holy days.

2.6 Morality in sport

Fair competition

Most religious believers regard fair play and **honesty** as essential in sport. But dishonesty is a continual problem as some competitors are so motivated that they are prepared to do almost anything to win. For example:

- In football some players try to trick the referee into thinking that they have been fouled so that an opponent is booked or sent off or a penalty kick is awarded.
- In rugby, players may try to stamp on an opponent in the ruck (scrum), to try to injure their opponents.

In almost any sport, competitors may employ tactics such as distracting an opponent, or provoking them verbally. This is known as gamesmanship and considered by some as cheating. Religious believers encourage sportsmanship. For example, in cricket if a batsman hits the ball and is caught, he should immediately walk off and not wait at the crease for the umpire's decision.

> **Objectives**
> Consider morality in sport.

A Some players pretend to have been fouled

Use of money

Money can be used to gain an advantage and erode **fair competition**. Football teams like Manchester United or Chelsea have vast amounts of money to spend on buying players and paying their wages, whereas many other football teams have to sell their best players to survive. In Formula One motor racing some teams have a vastly superior budget to others. How can the teams with less money hope to compete?

At international level, some countries spend millions on providing excellent facilities for training, top coaches, state-of-the-art equipment and excellent nutrition. This gives competitors from those countries a tremendous advantage over those from less economically developed nations.

> **Key terms**
> **Honesty**: truthful. Not lying or cheating.
> **Fair competition**: where the contestants have a more-or-less equal chance to win.

Use of technology and science

How far should we go in order to win? There are many instances where science and technology are used in sport to gain an advantage over others. For example:

- Special clothing is produced to reduce water resistance for competitive swimmers.
- Designers spend millions developing faster and faster cars for motor racing.
- Athletes train overseas at high altitudes in order to perform better at sea level.
- Special diets to develop muscle are followed by most athletes and team players.

At the top level, sport has become a serious business. Nonetheless, at the amateur level, many people still take part in sports for fun and relaxation.

Modesty

The question of modesty and dress codes in sport is important for many religious believers. For example, strict Muslims believe that those who take part in sports such as athletics and swimming wear kit that is too revealing. This is classed as obscene and is considered a disgrace.

According to Shari'ah Law (Muslim religious law), it is not permitted to uncover certain parts of the body in public. For men, this means that the area between the knees and bellybutton must be covered, which makes it difficult to participate in sports such as sumo wrestling. For women, within strict Muslim communities, it means they must not reveal the shape of their bodies, which makes it hard for them to participate in most sports. In the past, Iranian women have only been able to compete in pistol and rifle shooting in the Olympics, and women in Saudi Arabia are not allowed to take part in any sports activity. Sporting activities involving both genders competing together are not allowed in Islam.

Other Muslims are not so strict about the dress code. For example, Susi Susanti was the first Olympic athlete to win a gold medal for Indonesia in badminton, and Algeria's Hassiba Boulmerka won the 1,500 metres in 1992, wearing contemporary running shorts.

B *Mixed sports or men and women training together is not normally allowed in Islam*

Summary

You should now be able to discuss morality in sport, including the importance for religious believers of honesty and the problems associated with fairness and modesty.

Discussion activity

With a partner, in a small group or as a class, discuss whether you agree with the idea that sport has become too competitive, with the result that there is now more gamesmanship, less sportsmanship and too much science and technology. Make notes on the opinions given and the reasons for them.

Activities

1. 'Everyone should have the same opportunity to win.' What do you think? Explain your opinion.

2. Explain Muslim attitudes towards modesty in sport.

AQA Examiner's tip

Make sure that you understand that religious believers believe in honesty, trust, equality and treating people with respect in sport.

Extension activity

Use the internet to research the sporting achievements of Hassiba Boulmerka, and of Ruqaya Al Ghasara, who ran the 200 metres in the Beijing Olympics.

2.7 Performance-enhancing drugs

> ... the use of doping agents in sport is both unhealthy and contrary to the ethics of sport ... it is necessary to protect the physical and spiritual health of athletes, the values of fair play and competition, the integrity and unity of sport, and the rights of those who take part in it at whatever level.
>
> *The International Olympic Committee*

Objectives

Consider the issues around the use of performance enhancing drugs.

What do performance-enhancing drugs do?

Type of drug	Examples	Uses
To build mass	Anabolic steroids Beta-2 agonists Human growth hormone (HGH)	Accelerates growth of muscle and body mass. Assists, for example, weightlifters, swimmers, rowers and sprinters.
Stimulants	Caffeine Amphetamines	Increases alertness, reduces tiredness and allows athletes to perform at their optimum level.
Sedatives	Beta blockers Marijuana	Helps calm the nerves. Sometimes used by archers or snooker players where they need steady hands.
Pain killers	Ibuprofen Acetaminophen	Enables training or competing beyond the pain barrier. Assists long-distance athletes.
To increase delivery of oxygen to the blood	Erythropietin (EPO) Oxyglobin	Increases stamina by boosting oxygen-carrying red blood cells. Used by cyclists and long-distance runners.
Masking drugs	Epitestosterone	Used to prevent the detection of other drugs. New ones are being developed all the time to aid drug cheats.

A Types of performance-enhancing drugs and their purposes

The risks

People who use **performance-enhancing drugs** run the risk of being found out. There is testing to catch cheats, and those caught face being shamed and banned from their sport.

Performance-enhancing drugs are dangerous because of their side effects. For example, anabolic steroids may cause jaundice, liver damage, mood swings, depression and aggression. In males they cause baldness, infertility and breast development; in women they stimulate hair growth on the face and body, cause deepening of the voice and possible infertility.

Key terms

Performance-enhancing drugs: substances used by those involved in sport to improve their performance. This practice is illegal and is a form of cheating.

Why do people take the risk?

Users of performance-enhancing drugs hope to gain an advantage over their opponents in order to steal the prize. The top sports people receive fame and fortune, so some people are prepared to take the risk.

Religious beliefs about performance-enhancing drugs

The six major religions are all against taking performance-enhancing drugs because it is:

- dishonourable
- cheating (seeking to gain an unfair advantage over the other competitors)
- stealing (obtaining money dishonestly if a prize or sponsorship is won)
- illegal (against the law)
- dangerous (damaging the health of the user).

What should happen to drug cheats?

Case study

Asafa Powell

Former world record holder for the 100 metres, Asafa Powell, said that those athletes who test positive for performance-enhancing drugs should be given a prison sentence. He is quoted as saying, 'If someone comes out and they are taking drugs and win the gold, they are robbing me of my gold medal. When people do things like that, they should be punished for it. Two years from the sport and then back, it is pretty easy. It's for the experts to see what else they can do about it and make the athletes understand. They should be given the impression that they will go to jail if they do it.'

Asafa Powell

Dwain Chambers

British athlete, Dwain Chambers, wished to be forgiven for taking performance-enhancing drugs and to be allowed to represent England in the 2008 Olympics. In October 2003 he failed a drug test having taken the performance-enhancing anabolic steroid THG. Dwain had equalled the British 100 metres record of 9.87 seconds and was the European champion in 2002. He was banned from taking part in the Olympics for life and all athletic competitions for two years. The International Association of Athletics Federation told him to repay £180,000 prize money and they took away his European gold medal and British record.

Dwain returned to competitive running after his ban and won the 2008 Olympic trials in a time of 10.00 seconds, but the courts refused to lift his Olympic ban.

B *Should Dwain Chambers be allowed to compete for Britain?*

Discussion activity

With a partner, in a small group or as a class, discuss the attitude of Asafa Powell and the case of Dwain Chambers. Consider whether drug cheats should be punished this severely or given a second chance? Make notes on the opinions given and the reasons for them.

Activities

Write an answer to the following questions:

1. 'Drug cheats should never be allowed to compete again.' Do you agree? Explain your opinion.

2. Explain why religious believers are against the use of performance-enhancing drugs.

3. 'It's the taking part that is important; it doesn't matter who wins.' What do you think? Explain your opinion.

AQA Examiner's tip

Make sure that you are able to explain why people are tempted to use performance-enhancing drugs, what effects they have and why religious believers and others oppose their use.

Summary

You should now be able to explain the use of performance-enhancing drugs in sport and why religious believers are opposed to their use.

2.8 Sports fans

The devotion of fans

Supporting a sports club or team becomes a dominant part of some peoples' lives – almost like a religion. Most religious believers stress the importance of getting things in the right perspective and putting God before sport, but much of the following can be said to copy religion.

Songs

Sports fans support their teams by singing or chanting during matches. Some teams have their own special anthems, adapt famous songs or take one from a musical. For example, West Ham supporters sing 'I'm forever blowing bubbles'. At football matches you are likely to hear:

'And it's [team's name]

[team's name] FC

They're by far the greatest team

The world has ever seen!'

Fans sing songs like this from the terraces or stands, even if their team is in a low league. Sometimes there are special songs sung against local rivals at derby matches or, if a team is losing, the opposition fans will break into:

'You're not singing, you're not singing any more!'

Memorabilia

Sports and leisure **memorabilia** is big business. Leading auction houses, such as Christie's, Bonhams and Sotherby's, sell many collectable items. The autographs of stars like Tiger Woods and Robbie Williams and Hollywood actors are extremely popular. Fans from around the world love to obtain signed shirts, photographs and programmes, and are prepared to pay large sums for the genuine article.

Mementos

Mementos are also very popular. Club shops are stocked with items containing the brand name and logo, including scarves, watches, notepads and pens. Supporters enjoy displaying the colours of their teams and having shirts or videos to remind them of special occasions, such as winning the league.

Pilgrimage

Christians have supported football since it began. Some of the Premier teams, such as Everton, evolved from church teams, and Liverpool started as a Wesley Methodist team. However, some say that football commands such support that it has become like a religion. There are certain similarities with religion in the way fans behave. Around the world, billions of people follow football on television, and hundreds of thousands make the 'pilgrimage' to football grounds on match days

Objectives

Investigate the devotion of fans, and how they support their teams.

Key terms

Memorabilia: a collection of memorable things linked to a particular person or sport.

Mementos: souvenirs.

A Sports memorabilia, such as autographed football shirts is big business

Extension activity

Use the internet to find out more about what is being bought and sold as sports memorabilia and record examples of the prices being paid.

> *Someone said 'football is more important than life and death to you' and I said 'Listen, it's more important than that'.*
>
> Bill Shankly, former manager of Liverpool Football Club (Source: Granada Television chat show, 1981)

Chapter 2 Religion, sport and leisure 45

to watch it in person. Some fans spend thousands of pounds each year on purchasing season tickets and travel to the away games. Many supporters of the top clubs try to get tickets for the Champions League or the Union of European Football Associations (UEFA) Cup away matches, which are being held in other European countries. Fanatical support also applies to supporters of other sports and leisure activities, such as fans flocking to concerts to see their favourite musicians and singers, or making a pilgrimage to his or her birthplace.

links
Look back to pages 32 and 33 for a comparison with religious pilgrimages.

Fan or fanatic?
Some fans go to extraordinary lengths to support their team. Les McKee often travelled from Ireland to see his team, Liverpool, play at Anfield but he was so passionate about his team that he wanted he see every match. So, he gave up everything at home, sold his belongings and moved to Liverpool with £500 and some clothes. With no job for months, he had to sleep on friend's floors until he found employment and accommodation. His heart was at Anfield and he was prepared to do anything to be in a position to watch his team.

Case study

Symbols
Symbols are used to represent different sports or clubs. Often clubs have nicknames: Plymouth Argyle FC is known as the 'Pilgrims,' and Norwich City as the 'Canaries'. The names of animals or colours are popular. Even national teams are given nicknames. In Rugby League, the Russian team is known as the 'Bears' and the Australian team as the 'Kangaroos'. Clubs have logos which reflect the sport and often their background and nicknames.

B *Some fans paint team or national colours on their body*

Research activity
Use the internet and the library to find out about the symbol of the Olympic Games. Why are there five intertwined rings and what is the significance of the colours?

Discussion activity
With a partner, in a small group or as a class discuss whether you agree that sport has become like a religion, with its own songs, memorabilia, mementos and pilgrimages. Make notes on the opinions given and the reasons for them.

AQA Examiner's tip
Make sure you are able to explain how fans show support for their favourite teams and why some people think that following a team can become almost a religion.

Activities
1. Give three ways fans might show devotion to their favourite sport or team.
2. 'Football isn't a matter of life and death – it's much more important than that!' What do you think? Explain your opinion.

Summary
You should now be able to explain how some fans show their devotion to their teams and how their support has almost become like a religion to them.

2.9 Support within sport and leisure

Chaplains in sport

Many teams have sports **chaplains** who provide pastoral care and spiritual support for the individual sportsperson or team, the backup staff and their families. Some sports stars find becoming famous and having thousands of fans, and huge sums of money, difficult to handle and need someone to talk to. In Britain, chaplains are mainly Christian and in 1991 the Baptist Church set up SCORE – an organisation that encourages and trains ministers to help sportspeople.

Christians in sport

The organisation Christians in Sport was officially set up in 1980 and has since developed internationally. It aims to:

- encourage Christians in sport to represent and share their faith
- support churches in preparing sportspeople to represent Christ
- train leaders.

Sport and leisure as big business

Enormous sums of money are spent on sport and leisure. This includes providing venues, equipment, accommodation, travel, covering production costs as well as paying the professionals. It is estimated that staging the Beijing Olympic Games in 2008 cost China £35 billion. In the UK, the 90,000 seat stadium at Wembley cost over £800 million. To stage an event like the Glastonbury Festival costs thousands of pounds. Ticket sales alone would not be sufficient to pay for such events, so the income is supplemented by finance obtained from, for example, TV deals, sponsorship and taxes. Religious believers might ask whether this is good stewardship (use) of money when millions in the world are so poor that they are struggling to get food to eat.

Pay

Sports **superstars** and the top clubs can become very wealthy. Individuals may be paid enormous salaries or obtain thousands of pounds in prize money, as well as earning millions from advertising and endorsements. In the 12 months from 1 June 2007 to 1 June 2008, it is estimated that the American golfer Tiger Woods earned £57 million and that footballer David Beckham earned approximately £25 million.

Many would argue that this sort of income is excessive and greedy when other professionals are struggling to make a living. Religious believers might ask whether these superstars become idols in peoples' lives. Others believe that superstars deserve to make a fortune because they are the best, and they have sacrificed many things to make it to the top. They give tremendous entertainment to society and are an inspiration to others.

Objectives

Consider the role of chaplains and Christians in sport.

Know about the financial backing given to sport and leisure.

Key terms

Chaplain: a priest, pastor, rabbi, imam or other member of the clergy who advises on moral, ethical and spiritual matters.

Superstar: a widely acclaimed celebrity, such as a film star or sports star, who has great popular appeal.

Sponsorship: the provision of financial or material assistance by a private enterprise or business in return for publicity.

Extension activity

1. Use the internet to find out more about the cost of the 2012 London Olympic Games.

A Top sports stars can earn vast sums of money, can this ever be justified?

Extension activity

2. Use the internet or library to find out some of the costs involved in making a Hollywood film, including the pay given to the acting superstars.

Sponsorship

Sponsorship is becoming more important in sport and leisure.

Sponsors benefit from:

- the publicity the company gains for its logo or brand name
- advertising opportunities through television, radio or newspaper coverage of an event
- a reduction in their tax bill
- the association with health and fitness
- increased sales of their products.

Risks to the sponsors include the event not being successful, the media losing interest or negative publicity if something goes wrong, such as through vandalism or drug taking.

The sports gain by:

- receiving extra finance to invest in equipment, facilities, staff and coaching
- receiving financial help to develop new technologies and young talent
- gaining higher profile, which helps them to attract talented players.

Risks include a sudden reduction in income if the sponsors withdraw, and the unfavourable conditions that might be imposed by the sponsors.

B *Formula One relies heavily on sponsorship*

Discussion activity

With a partner, in a small group or as a class, discuss whether you agree with the following statement:

'The amount of money superstars get paid is unfair and outrageous.'

Make notes on the opinions given and the reasons for them.

AQA Examiner's tip

Make sure you are able to explain what is involved in sponsorship and its advantages and disadvantages.

Activities

Answer the following questions:

1. Explain the role of chaplains and the aims of Christians in Sport.
2. Explain the advantages and disadvantages of sponsorship.
3. 'Too much money is being spent on leisure activities.' What do you think? Explain your opinion.

Summary

You should now be able to explain the role of chaplains and Christians in sport, and the financial support given to sport and leisure.

2.10 Issues of equality

Objectives
Investigate issues concerning equality in sport and leisure.

> *Exercise dissipates tension, and tension is the enemy of serenity. I found that I worked better and thought more clearly when I was in good physical condition, and so training became one of the inflexible disciplines in my life.*
>
> Nelson Mandela, former President of South Africa

According to Nelson Mandela, sport is a tremendous influence for good in the world. Men and woman throughout the world, able-bodied or not, **amateurs** or **professionals**, should all have an opportunity to demonstrate their sporting talent and enjoy sport. But is there equality in sport?

Gender differences

There is still inequality in the amount of money that top female sports athletes earn by comparison with their male counterparts. Is this fair? In 2008 Tiger Woods earned almost as much in one year as the top ten sportswomen combined. The highest paid women are golfers and tennis players. In football, the gap in pay between men and women is enormous and this is reflected in a much smaller number of female players and spectators.

In the past, some sports were exclusively practised by men or women. Nowadays, this is not so evident although there may not be professional leagues for one gender, for example in Rugby Union and Rugby League. In most sports men and women take part separately, but in others, such as show jumping, they compete on an equal basis. Some exclusively male sports clubs have come under attack from women who wish to become members and to have equal rights.

Amateur or professional

Participants in amateur sports do not get paid and participate during their leisure time. Amateurs may still take their sport seriously and attempt to become highly skilled, such as the teams who represent Britain in the rowing events in the Olympics. Youth teams and many adult teams take part for fun, social reasons, to improve a skill or to get fit, and not for money. The same applies in other leisure activities – so, unpaid actors may put on an amateur production. Often people turn professional when they become good at a sport and wish to make it their career. The income enables such professionals to have more time to train and become more skilled.

The Paralympic Games

In 1960 the first World Games for the Disabled were held in Rome and 23 countries took part. The competition proved to be a success and since then, like the Olympics, the games have taken place every four years and are now called The Paralympic Games. Thousands of disabled athletes from over 130 countries take part in events such as

Beliefs and teachings

Most religions teach that men and women are equal and many would argue that this should be the case in sport.

Buddhism 'The things which divide and separate people – race, religion, gender, social position – are all illusory.'
Dhammapada 6

Christianity 'There is neither Jew nor Greek, slave nor free, male nor female, for you are all one in Christ Jesus.'
Galatians 3:28

Hinduism 'I look upon all creatures equally.'
Bhagavad Gita 9.29

Islam 'Men and women were created from a single soul.'
Qur'an 4:1

'Men are the protectors and maintainers of women.'
Qur'an 4:34

Judaism 'So God created human beings, making them to be like himself. He created them male and female.'
Genesis 1:27

Sikhism All men and women are equal: 'we are the children of the One God'.
Guru Granth Sahib 611

A Amateur and professional golfers may compete in the same competition

running, swimming and wheelchair basketball. There are different categories for the athletes depending on the seriousness of their disability. Technology has made real progress in helping the athletes overcome their disabilities. For example, double amputee South African runner Oscar Pistorius, by using J-shaped carbon fibre blades, can now run almost as fast as the top able-bodied athletes.

B Wheelchair athlete competing in a wheelchair marathon

C Wheelchair basketball

Case study

'Super-athletes'

Swimmer Natalie du Toit lost her left leg in a road accident in 2001, but continued her swimming. In the 2004 Athens Paralympics she won five golds and a silver medal. So, she became the first athlete to compete at both the Paralympics and the Olympics by representing South Africa in the Beijing Olympics. She qualified for the Olympics by finishing fourth in the 10 kilometre race at the open water world championships, a remarkable feat.

Single-arm amputee Natalia Partyka also competed at the 2008 Olympics, representing Poland at table tennis in the team event.

Key terms

- **Amateur**: a person who performs or takes part in an activity as an unpaid pastime, rather than as a profession.
- **Professional**: a person who performs or takes part in an activity for payment.
- **Disability**: a physical incapacity caused by injury or disease.

Discussion activity

With a partner, in a small group or as a class discuss what you think Nelson Mandela meant by his quotation on page 48.

Activities

1. Explain the difference between amateur and professional status.
2. 'Men and women, able-bodied and disabled athletes should be allowed to compete on an equal basis in all sports.' What do you think? Explain your opinion.

Summary

You should now be able to explain that sport has the capacity to bring together people of different nationalities, genders and abilities, and that religious believers consider all human beings to be of equal worth.

AQA Examiner's tip

Make sure you are aware of the beliefs and teachings of the religion(s) you have studied concerning equality of the sexes.

Assessment guidance

2

Religion, sport and leisure – summary

For the examination you should now be able to:

- ✓ explain religious and other attitudes towards the purpose, use and importance of leisure
- ✓ demonstrate knowledge and understanding of religious and other attitudes to sport, and their practical application
- ✓ demonstrate knowledge and understanding of religious teachings that underpin such attitudes
- ✓ give a reasoned evaluation of beliefs and practices relating to sport and leisure
- ✓ explain the importance of morality in sport and issues relating to unfair practices
- ✓ explain the finances involved in leisure and sport
- ✓ explain and evaluate the ways fans show their devotion to their favourite sports.

Sample answer

1. Write an answer to the following exam question.

   'Sports superstars have become too greedy.' Do you agree?

   Give reasons for your answer, showing that you have thought about more than one point of view.

   (6 marks)

2. Read the following sample answer.

   > Sports superstars now get more money in a week than most people earn in a year. This cannot be right as many people are struggling to make enough money to live. Many of the clubs cannot afford to pay such high wages and so the best players try to get to those who can. This makes for unfair competition. The Buddha taught that it was wrong to crave for possessions and money. Desire causes much suffering so he taught people to live by the Middle Way (not in extreme poverty or a life of riches). This most superstars ignore and appear greedy to get every last pound they can although they are earning millions.

   > On the other hand, you could argue that if they were not worth a lot of money they would not be able to get it. After all, their career in sports is only likely to last a short period of time. By their mid thirties nearly all have finished their time at the top, and what if they get injured! They need to make provision for their futures and quite a lot of the money will be paid as taxes. Also, they may be tithing their money and giving large sums away to charity. Some Christians, for example, give one tenth of their income to the church or charity. This isn't being greedy.

3. With a partner, discuss the sample answer. Do you think that there are other things that the student could have included in the answer?

4. What mark (out of 6) would you give this answer? (Look at the mark scheme in the Introduction on page 7 (AO2) before you attempt this). What are the reasons for the mark you have given?

AQA Examination-style questions

1 Look at the photograph and answer the following questions.

(a) Give **two** reasons why relaxation is important. *(2 marks)*

(b) Explain briefly why most religious believers are concerned about gambling. *(3 marks)*

(c) 'Religious believers should encourage people to belong to a team.' What do you think? Explain your opinion. *(3 marks)*

(d) Explain the attitudes of religious believers towards the use of performance-enhancing drugs. *(4 marks)*

(e) 'Too many people treat sport like a religion.' Do you agree? Give reasons for your answer, showing that you have thought about more than one point of view. *(6 marks)*

> **AQA Examiner's tip**
> Remember that when you are asked if you agree with a statement, you must show what you think and the reasons why other people might take a different view. If your answer is one sided, you will only achieve a maximum of 4 marks. If you make no comment about religious belief or practice, you will achieve no more than 3 marks.

3 Religion and work

3.1 The purpose and importance of work

What is work?

Many people would say that **work** is their paid employment; for example, working as a teacher or in a factory. Work can also be voluntary and unpaid, such as completing tasks in class at school or looking after the home by doing the cooking and cleaning. The purpose of work includes making a positive contribution to society and providing for our needs.

Why work?

Work is important for a number of reasons including:

- It is necessary for survival: without someone working, there would be no money to buy food or clothing, or to provide a home, and nobody providing these necessities.
- It enables a person to contribute to the community and be a productive citizen and valued member of society.
- It gives a person a purpose in life and prevents boredom.
- It provides the opportunity for the development of new skills and the learning of new things.
- It gives a person self-respect, dignity and self-worth if he or she does a good job.
- For many, it provides the opportunity to socialise and gain friends.

Religion and work

The Genesis creation story in the Bible says that God worked for six days in creating the universe, and that he rested on the seventh day of the week (Saturday). Then God gave Adam the task of caring for the Garden of Eden.

> **Objectives**
> Understand why work is important.

A Time to work!

B A factory worker making jeans

> **Beliefs and teachings**
>
> And God blessed the seventh day and made it holy, because on it he rested from all the work of creating that he had done.
>
> *Genesis 2:3*
>
> The Lord God took the man and put him in the Garden of Eden to work it and take care of it.
>
> *Genesis 2:15*

Christians, Jews and Muslims believe that work is a duty given to them by God or Allah.

After Adam and Eve had disobeyed God by eating the forbidden fruit, their task got harder.

> **Key terms**
>
> **Work**: the physical or mental exertion in order to do, make or accomplish something.

> **AQA Examiner's tip**
>
> Learn a quotation from the religion(s) you have studied which shows why work is important.

Chapter 3 Religion and work

> **Beliefs and teachings**
>
> To Adam he said, 'Because you listened to your wife and ate from the tree about which I commanded you, 'You must not eat of it', cursed is the ground because of you; through painful toil you will eat of it all the days of your life.'
>
> *Genesis 3:17*

There are times when work does seem like a punishment. In the Old Testament, when Moses requested that the Israelites be allowed to leave the land, Pharaoh punished the Hebrews by requiring them to make more bricks, with fewer resources.

> **Beliefs and teachings**
>
> You are no longer to supply the people with straw for making bricks; let them go and gather their own straw.
>
> *Exodus 5:7*

However, completing a job successfully brings a sense of achievement and satisfaction. For example, Muslims believe that:

> **Beliefs and teachings**
>
> No one eats better food than that which they have earned by their own labours.
>
> *Hadith*

Buddhists believe in seeking constructive and helpful employment ('right livelihood') in order to develop abilities and skills and contribute to society in a helpful way.

> **Beliefs and teachings**
>
> And what is right livelihood? There is the case where a disciple of the noble ones, having abandoned dishonest livelihood, keeps his life going with right livelihood: this is called right livelihood.
>
> *Samyutta Nikaya 45.8*

Hindus say that work is a natural thing for humans to do because without it life would be dull, uninteresting and monotonous.

> **Beliefs and teachings**
>
> Perform your prescribed duty, for action is better than inaction. A man cannot even maintain his physical body without work.
>
> *Bhagavad Gita 3:8*

Sikhs recognise how important work is in order to support their families.

> **Beliefs and teachings**
>
> The farmers love to work their farms; they plough and work the fields, so that their sons and daughters may eat.
>
> *Guru Granth Sahib 166*

C A father and son showing the vegetables they have grown

Discussion activity

With a partner, in a small group or as a class, discuss whether you agree with the following descriptions of work.

'Work is: vital; creative; a punishment; healthy. Work prevents boredom.'

List the different descriptions and make notes on the opinions given.

Activities

1. Explain why work is important.

2. Explain what the religion(s) you have studied teach about the need to work.

3. 'God made us for work.' What do you think? Explain your opinion.

Summary

You should now be able to explain the purpose and importance of work, and religious attitudes regarding the need to work.

3.2 Careers and vocation

Careers

We live in a changing world. Gone are the days when most people stayed in one job for their entire **career**. It is, however, important to plan a career in order to obtain the necessary qualifications to obtain a rewarding job.

Vocation

Christians believe that God has a purpose in life for every individual. Orthodox and Roman Catholic Christians in particular associate the idea of **vocation** with a divine call to work in the Church, for example as a priest. In a broader sense, religious believers refer to vocation as the opportunity to use their gifts for the good of everyone in whatever job or profession they practise.

Objectives

Investigate the importance of having a career and the jobs religions regard as unacceptable.

Understand what is meant by a vocation.

Extension activity

1. Connexions is an organisation that helps people choose a career. Use the internet to find out more about its work.

Case study

Jackie Pullinger

In 1966 Jackie Pullinger left Britain on a one-way boat ticket to Hong Kong. This Christian woman, in her early twenties, believed that God had called her to work in one of the most dangerous spots in the world. She became a music teacher in the Walled City – an area where even the police were too frightened to go. This was the home of criminals, drug addicts, prostitutes and Triad gangs. People lived amongst the rubbish, open sewers and rats. Although fearful for her own safety, she began to tell these people about the love of Jesus. At first they did not listen to her, but she began to help the most desperate people by giving them food, medical care and shelter. She gradually gained the trust of even the Triad gang members and she helped many break free from the terrible grip of heroin and opium addiction. She prayed for those addicted. When they came off the drugs straightaway without any problems, they claimed this was because of the power of God. With her friends, Jackie formed the St Stephen's Society, which runs one of the most successful drug rehabilitation programmes in the world. Its work has expanded to the Philippines and Thailand. In Hong Kong the Walled City has been knocked down, but Jackie's work continues as she regards it as her vocation.

A *Jackie Pullinger*

The Dalai Lama

Buddhists believe Tenzin Gyatso is the fourteenth reincarnation of the Dalai Lama, and as such has the task of spreading a message of peace and compassion throughout the world. At the age of 16, during the time of conflict with China, he became Head of State for Tibet. In 1959, when the Chinese military took over Tibet, he was forced to leave the country and live in exile in India. He is the Tibetan spiritual leader and has travelled widely, meeting heads of state and spiritual leaders. In recognition of his efforts for peace he was awarded the Nobel Peace Prize in 1989. He often says that he is just a simple Buddhist monk.

B *The Dalai Lama*

Extension activity

2 Find out more about Jackie Pullinger, or the Dalai Lama, by using the internet or a library. Alternatively, research the life and work of someone from the religion(s) you have studied who claimed to have a vocation.

Key terms

Career: way of making a living, often in a profession.

Vocation: a career which the individual feels called to by God.

Unacceptable professions

Religious believers see some careers as unacceptable.

Beliefs and teachings

Buddhists believe that:

A lay follower should not engage in five types of business. Which five? Business in weapons, business in human beings, business in meat, business in intoxicants, and business in poison.

Anguttara Nikaya 5.177

Christians are not allowed to take on any job that promotes immorality, for example anything pornographic, or is associated with the New Age movement or the occult, such as horoscopes, witchcraft or spiritualism. Jobs that involve dishonesty or the gambling industry are not acceptable to Christians.

Most Hindus are vegetarians and believe it wrong to hurt other beings. Unacceptable work includes pornography and working at an abattoir.

For Muslims, companies that produce haram (forbidden) products or are against Islamic teaching are not permitted. These include breweries, casinos, dance halls and anything related to prostitution, pornography or statue making.

Jews are not involved in farming animals, such as pigs, that are not 'kosher'.

For Khalsa Sikhs, professions involving alcohol and tobacco, gambling, the production of meat, the cutting of hair and pornography are unacceptable.

C *Many religious believers would not work in the alcohol industry*

Discussion activity

With a partner, in a small group or as a class debate whether you think Jackie Pullinger was just naïve, very foolish, 'called by God', or extremely brave to go to Hong Kong's Walled City.

AQA Examiner's tip

Ensure that you are able to write about the life and work of someone who believes that they have a vocation in life.

Activities

1 Explain why giving careful consideration to a future career is important.

2 Explain what is meant by a 'vocation'.

3 'Do well in the GCSE exams and you will have a good career.' What do you think of this statement? Explain your opinion.

Summary

You should now be able to explain the importance of careers, vocations and the jobs that religions believe are unacceptable.

3.3 Business and enterprise

The nature of business

A **business** may also be called a company, a firm or an **enterprise**. The purpose is to provide goods or services to individuals or other businesses or companies. Businesses are divided into public and private sector businesses. Public sector means those owned by the government and paid for out of taxes; for example, the police, the armed forces and most hospitals and schools. Private sector means that the businesses are owned by private individuals. These owners or operators of businesses wish to obtain a financial return and earn a profit. This is in return for the work they do and the goods or services they provide to their customers. This usually involves a certain amount of risk: if they do not make a profit, they may cease to trade or go bankrupt.

> **Objectives**
>
> Understand the importance of business and enterprise.
>
> Investigate religious attitudes to work and business.

A At one end of the scale, mining produces raw materials for other businesses to make things

B Design and research carried out on computers is at the other end of the scale

Religious believers' attitudes to business

Most religious believers support business and enterprise because they regard work and business practice as essential. Conducting oneself honestly in business is often seen as a form of worship, and prayer. Most religious believers condemn sharp practices and deceit. Jobs that are constructive and helpful to society are regarded as acceptable professions. All the caring professions, such as nursing and teaching, and the production of essential goods, or manufacturing, would be regarded as important work. Employment that shows little or no value for the individual or for society, is not acceptable. Buddhists, for example, would regard the production of weapons as an unacceptable profession because they are against violence (First Precept). Buddhists believe in following the Middle Way, so business is important, providing the environment is respected and the temptation to become greedy is resisted.

> **Research activity**
>
> Research the local newspapers, telephone directories and community websites to find businesses in the school area. Look at a range of organisations large and small, private and public, and record examples of each and the type of work they do. What types are most numerous in your area? Might any be regarded as 'unacceptable' by a religion?

Christians believe in living out their faith, giving glory to God, in the whole of their lives, which includes their working lives. This means that honesty should be shown in all business transactions and work.

Beliefs and teachings

Whatever you do, work at it with all your heart, as working for the Lord, not for men.

Colossians 3:23

Hindus teach that honest work and business are praise and a prayer to god. As Hinduism is a way of life, there is no distinction between the religious part of a believer's life and the other parts, such as business and work.

Muslims believe that work is an obligation (a duty) and an act of worship, and Allah's help is given to those who work in business and strive (make an effort) with commitment.

Beliefs and teachings

As for those who strive in our cause, we will surely guide them in our paths. Most assuredly, GOD is with the pious.

Qur'an 29:69

Jews believe that God allows people to have good business opportunities:

Beliefs and teachings

But remember the LORD your God, for it is he who gives you the ability to produce wealth, and so confirms his covenant.

Deuteronomy 8:18

Sikhs emphasise the importance of working with all their talents and abilities, using their hands, their intellect and their hearts in the service of themselves, their family and the community. Members of the Khalsa pray before starting work.

Beliefs and teachings

My own occupation is to work to praise the Lord.

Guru Granth Sahib 1331

Activities

1. Explain what is meant by acceptable and unacceptable work.
2. Explain why some religious believers say that work is a form of worship or prayer.
3. 'Religious believers should be concerned about spiritual things, not business and enterprise.' What do you think?
   Explain your opinion.

Key terms

Business: a commercial or industrial firm. Sometimes, business refers to the occupation, work or trade in which a person is engaged.

Enterprise: a project or task that requires boldness or effort and a willingness to try new approaches or actions.

AQA Examiner's tip

Make sure you know what the religion(s) you are studying believe about business and the value of work.

Discussion activity

With a partner, in a small group or as a class, discuss whether you think that every student should be taught about business and enterprise. Make notes on the opinions given.

links

To find out more about the opinion of religious believers regarding specific businesses or professions, see page 55.

Summary

You should now be able to explain what is meant by business and enterprise, and religious attitudes to them.

3.4 The economy and taxation

The national economy

The **economy** is about buying and selling goods or services. To make the economy work, people need something to sell what others are prepared to buy. For example, a baker provides bread to his or her customers either through his or her own shop or through another outlet. In Britain, there is a 'mixed economy' or, in other words, a mixture of private businesses or companies that respond to consumer demand and public services provided by national or local government paid for through the **taxation** system. These public services include education and healthcare. If people are enterprising and produce and buy goods, then the economy is likely to grow, but this depends partly on the world economy, international trade, interest rates and government policy. Increases in the cost of fuel or interest rates, increased unemployment or loss of confidence in the economy can cause a slowdown, which can develop into a recession (when the overall economy declines).

Objectives

Investigate what is meant by the economy.

Understand why taxes are necessary.

Know religious attitudes towards money and tithing.

Key terms

Economy: the system by which the production, distribution and consumption of goods and services is organised in a country. The generation of wealth through business and industry.

Taxation: the method by which the government receives an income; for example, from income tax, Value Added Tax (VAT), inheritance tax.

Tithes: the giving of a tenth of your income to God.

A *The government takes taxes from people's wages*

B *Tax is paid on petrol*

Taxation

The Chancellor of the Exchequer works out a budget for the government's spending. Part of a person's earnings is taken in taxes to pay for such things as schools, the National Health Service, defence, law and order and social services. If the government wishes to give more money to education, then the other services have to receive less, or taxes will rise. Without taxation free or subsidised services would not be available; for example, students would have to pay for their education or there would be no schools.

Direct taxation is when money is taken out of a person's salary. These taxes include income tax and National Insurance. The more a person earns, the more tax is taken before the worker receives his or her pay.

Indirect taxation is charged on goods and services. For most items that we buy, Value Added Tax (VAT) is added, but essentials like most food and children's clothing are exempt. There are taxes on cigarettes, alcohol and petrol. If a person inherits property, they may have to pay inheritance tax. Businesses pay corporation tax, which is charged on the profits they make.

Money from earning and tithes

Jews and Christians believe that wages should be spent wisely to support the family and those in need. Some Jews and Christians pay a **tithe** (a voluntary tax or levy) to support their synagogue or church, or the work of a religious organisation. In the past, part may have been paid 'in kind' (such as produce from a farm), but today tithes are usually given in the form of money.

> ### Beliefs and teachings
>
> A tithe of everything from the land, whether grain from the soil or fruit from the trees, belongs to the LORD.
>
> *Leviticus* 27:30

St Paul taught the early Christians that it is important to pay taxes to enable the government to do their job.

> ### Beliefs and teachings
>
> This is also why you pay taxes, for the authorities are God's servants, who give their full time to governing. Give everyone what you owe him: if you owe taxes, pay taxes; if revenue, then revenue.
>
> *Romans* 13:6–7

Muslims are obliged to pay 'zakat' (one of the Five Pillars). This is 2.5 per cent of a person's surplus wealth when all the essentials have been paid. The money is used for the upkeep of the mosque, the spread of Islam and to help those in need. Muslims believe that Allah provides wealth and consequently that it should be spent with care. Spending money on gambling is not allowed.

Buddhists, Hindus and Sikhs believe that generosity and compassion have a positive affect on a person's karma. Sikhs believe that they should work honestly and use some of their wages to help those in need. Hindus say that disabled and sick people should be exempt from paying taxes.

> ### Beliefs and teachings
>
> A blind man, an idiot (a cripple) who moves with the help of a board, a man full seventy years old … shall not be compelled by any to pay a tax.
>
> *Laws of Manu* 8.394

AQA Examiner's tip
Be prepared to write about why people pay taxes.

Discussion activity
With a partner, in a small group or as a class, discuss whether you agree that unless you are young, sick, old or disabled you cannot be a good citizen unless you pay taxes. Make notes on the opinions given and the reasons for them.

Activities
1. Explain what is meant by the economy of a country.
2. Explain why some people tithe.
3. 'There are too many taxes.' What do you think? Give your opinion.

Summary
You should now be able to explain how the economy works and understand basic facts about a taxation system.

3.5 Rights and responsibilities: employers

Employers' rights and responsibilities

Employers may be responsible for one **employee**, or for many thousands. At one end of the scale, a shopkeeper may wish to hire someone to give himself or herself a break for a couple of hours a day and, at the other end of the scale, the largest companies have thousands of full-time employees. Employers have a right to expect honesty, effort and loyalty from their employees. They need to balance interests such as ensuring that the wage bill is not too high, with achieving high productivity from the workforce. Without this balance, the company is unlikely to make a profit and this could result in staff being made redundant or the firm going out of business. Employers have a duty, however, to pay their employees a **fair wage**, which in the UK is at least the national minimum wage.

> **Objectives**
>
> Investigate the rights, responsibilities and expectations of employers.
>
> Examine the need for health and safety measures.

Case study: Holiday camp workers

Workers employed at a holiday camp had a monthly sum deducted from their wages. The employer argued that this was to pay for their accommodation and heating bills while they were employed at the camp. This meant, however, that many staff members received less than the national minimum wage. The case was taken to the Employment Appeals Tribunal, which ruled in favour of the employees.

Code of conduct

Employers expect employees to follow the company's **code of conduct**. This includes, for example, being committed to maintaining confidentiality about commercial information and customers' and suppliers' details. Maintaining high principles of honesty, dealing honourably with clients and showing a duty of care (for example, looking after other employees) are other aspects of such codes. Acting professionally, treating men and women equally, and other discrimination issues are covered by a company's code of conduct.

A Employees in the UK are entitled to be paid at least the national minimum wage

Health and safety

Employers also have a duty to look after the **health and safety** of their employees and to follow the guidance contained in law concerning employment, such as the 1974 Health and Safety at Work Act.

Case study: Morecambe Bay tragedy

In 2004 a terrible tragedy took place in Morecambe Bay, when 23 Chinese workers lost their lives. No risk assessment had been undertaken and no health and safety measures were in place. The workers were harvesting cockles on the dangerous tidal banks. They did not notice the rising tide until it was too late, and they drowned.

> **links**
>
> Find out more about the national minimum wage on page 63.

> **Extension activity**
>
> Use the internet or library to find out more about the 1974 Health and Safety at Work Act. Make notes on some of the main provisions made by the Act.

The Health and Safety Executive (HSE) has the task of promoting health and safety for employees:

> Our mission is to protect people's health and safety by ensuring risks in the changing workplace are properly controlled.
>
> Health and Safety Executive (HSE). Crown Copyright

Under the 1995 Reporting of Injuries, Diseases and Dangerous Occurrences Regulation (RIDDOR), employers must record and report to the HSE some work-related accidents. These include deaths, major injuries, injuries where the employee is unable to work for three consecutive days and dangerous occurrences where an injury has been narrowly avoided.

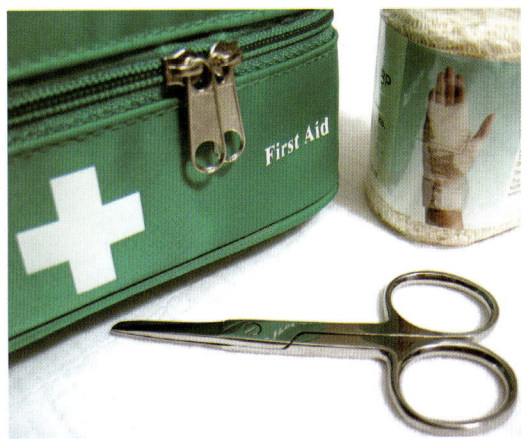

Key terms

Employer: a person or firm that employs (hires) workers.

Employee: a person who works for another in return for wages.

Fair wage: appropriate pay for the time, effort and skill given to the job.

Code of conduct: a set of principles and expectations that are considered binding on any person who is working for the company.

Health and Safety: issues concerning the protection of employees.

B Well-maintained fire extinguishers and first aid kits are essential to health and safety in the workplace

Research activity

Using the internet or a library, research the statistics concerning accidents at work and find incidents where workers have suffered because health and safety rules were broken.

Discussion activity

With a partner, in a small group or as a class, discuss the following statement:

'Health and safety at work is an issue that is not taken seriously enough.' Make notes on the opinions given and the reasons for them.

Activities

1. Explain what employers have a right to expect from their workforce.
2. Explain what is being done to protect workers.
3. 'If people followed religious teachings there would be no need for a code of conduct.' What do you think? Explain your opinion.

AQA Examiner's tip

Make sure you understand that you cannot have rights without responsibilities, and that this applies to both employers and employees.

Summary

You should now be able to discuss the rights and responsibilities of employers, including the need for a code of conduct and health and safety measures.

3.6 Rights and responsibilities: employees

Employees' rights and responsibilities

There are different types of employees; for example, those who work full time, those who work part time, and permanent and temporary employees.

All employees have a responsibility not to cheat their employer by, for example, doing the minimal amount of work or making long-distance, personal phone calls using the company phone. Job descriptions set out the responsibilities and state what is expected of an employee. Failure to take these responsibilities seriously can result in a pay cut, or even dismissal. Employees also have a responsibility towards other workers. Discrimination, harassment and bullying can result in a court case.

Government legislation, such as The Employment Rights Act (1996), The Sex Discrimination Act (1975), The Disability Discrimination Act (1995) and The Employment Relations Acts (1999 and 2003), specifies a range of rights for employees. These include:

- a **contract** containing the terms and conditions of employment
- protection against unfair dismissal
- the right to have an itemised pay statement
- protection against gender and racial discrimination (including equal pay, job advertisements, promotion and training)
- the right to belong to a trade union
- protection against religious discrimination
- maternity rights and parental leave
- time off for public duty, such as jury service.

Objectives

Examine the rights and responsibilities of employees.

Investigate what is meant by 'fair wages'.

Key terms

Contract: an agreement concerning the responsibilities and conditions of work between employer and employee.

Minimum wage: the national minimum wage is the lowest hourly rate that it is legal for an employer to pay to employees or workers.

Family commitments: the need to look after the family.

A Employees are entitled to a lunch break

links

The term 'fair wage' is introduced and defined on page 60, or you can look it up in the Glossary at the back of this book.

Fair wages

The Universal Declaration of Human Rights (1948) states that workers have the right to a fair wage, but in the past some employers exploited their workers by giving them unjustifiably low pay. In order to prevent this, the Government introduced the National Minimum Wage Act. It first took effect on 1 April 1999, and it was estimated that 1.5 million British workers benefited from it.

Advantages of a **minimum wage**:

- It gives workers a fair wage and prevents exploitation.
- It increases the standard of living for the poorest and most vulnerable.
- It gives a greater incentive for people to find work.

Disadvantages of a minimum wage:

- An employer might not be able to afford the National Minimum Wage as it reduces profit margins.
- It may, therefore, increase unemployment.
- Some employers may move their businesses to other countries where there is no minimum wage legislation.

Work–life balance

Work is getting more competitive, with higher and higher targets being set. It is difficult at times to ensure that work does not take over a person's life completely. There needs to be a life outside paid work to achieve a work–life balance, so a person is not working too long hours. Many workers have **family commitments** (to, for example, a wife, husband or partner, children or parents), and it is important to spend time with them. Religious believers support the idea that children need love, care and attention from parents. Relationships need to be worked at or they break down, and so families suffer.

Discussion activity

With a partner, in a small group or as a class, discuss how difficult you think it is to get the work–life balance right so people can both achieve and enjoy life. Make notes on the opinions given and the reasons for them.

Research activity

Use the library or the internet to find out how the National Minimum wage varies according to the employee's age, and research the different rules that apply. Record your findings and how much it is for the different groups.

B How difficult is it to get the work-life balance right to ensure a good quality of life?

Activities

1. Give three types of employee.
2. Explain the rights and responsibilities of employees.
3. 'All religious believers should be in favour of a National Minimum Wage.' What do you think? Give your opinion.

links

For more about achieving the work–life balance right, see pages 32–33.

AQA Examiner's tip

Make sure that you can explain why employees have responsibilities as well as rights.

Summary

You should now be able to explain the rights and responsibilities of employees, and the need to have fair wages.

3.7 Trade unions

What do trade unions do?

A **trade union** is a society of workers, formed to protect and improve their interests. Most employees pay to join a trade union for the benefits and protection it gives them. A union's function is to:

- negotiate with employers to try to get better pay or ensure fair wages
- ensure good working conditions, including adequate health and safety provision
- provide members with a training programme
- give members advice and support during a dispute with the management. This may include legal representation if required.

Unions may ballot members about strike action if they feel that the employers are being unreasonable, and they may campaign for the government to bring in legislation which would benefit their members. The majority of trade unions belong to the Trades Union Congress (TUC).

Objectives
Understand the need for and work of trade unions.

Investigate religious discrimination at work.

Key terms
Trade union: organisations that look after the interests of a group of workers.

A Trade unions ensure health and safety regulations are stuck to

B Trade unions may encourage workers to strike

In countries where there are few trade unions, where those that do exist are weak, or if there are few laws to protect workers, some employers take advantage of their employees. This can lead to terrible working conditions, including long hours and cramped, unhygienic workplaces. It can also lead to horrific accidents (see first case study). Many of the employees in these businesses, often called sweatshops, are children who are forced to work extremely long hours for little or no pay. In countries such as Bangladesh there have been reports of workers having to sew for 14 hours a day, 7 days a week. Wages are also very low, amounting to about 10 pence per hour, and are often paid weeks after they are due.

Extension activity
1. Use the internet or library to find out more about so called sweatshops and the conditions under which young people are expected to work.

Chapter 3 Religion and work

Case study: Tragedy in Morocco

At least 55 people were burned alive at a mattress and furniture factory in Casablanca, Morocco, in 2008. The owners and government officials had ignored the fact that many regulations were being broken at the factory. It is said that workers were not only paid less than the minimum wage, but that they worked in terrible conditions. Windows and doors were locked during working hours, with the result that no one could escape the fire. The fire extinguishers that existed were empty.

Extension activity

2 Use the internet, or a library, to research the work of one trade union, such as Unison, OR the history and work of the TUC.

Religion or belief discrimination?

Employers are not allowed to discriminate against a person because of his or her religion. Employment law defines religion or belief as any religion, religious belief or similar philosophical belief. However, if a specific religion is required for a particular job, this is allowed. To refuse a Sikh or a Hindu a job just because of his or her religious faith is not permitted, nor is consistently bullying someone because of what they believe. Someone in this situation could obtain help from his or her trade union.

AQA Examiner's tip

Make sure that you can evaluate the importance of the work of trade unions, and give examples of what they do.

Case study: Religious dress

Fifty-five-year-old Nadia Eweida of Twickenham, London, was sent on unpaid leave because British Airways bosses said she could not visibly wear her tiny cross at the check-in counter. She complained, saying that that Muslim women were allowed to wear a 'hijab' and Sikhs to wear turbans – both symbols of their religions. Eventually, after church leaders supported Miss Eweida, British Airways gave in to her request and allowed her to wear her cross.

C Should workers be allowed to wear a religious symbol?

Discussion activity

With a partner, in a small group or as a class, discuss whether or not trade unions are necessary in Britain in the 21st century. Make notes on the opinions given and the reasons for them.

Activities

1 Explain the work of trade unions.

2 Explain what is meant by 'poor conditions' at work.

3 'Religious believers, like the woman in case study 2, should be allowed to wear whatever religious symbol they like at work.' Give reasons for your answer, showing that you have thought about more than one point of view.

Summary

You should now be able to explain how trade unions look after their members' interests, and help them to protect their rights.

3.8 Voluntary work and service

Objectives
Investigate voluntary work in Britain.

Examine religious attitudes towards voluntary work and service.

A *Eight helping hands*

B *The more help, the easier it gets*

What is the importance of voluntary work?

Thousands of citizens in Britain take part in **voluntary work**. Some do so as individuals, others join groups to work together on a shared interest, normally for the benefit of others. There are more than 200,000 different **voluntary organisations** in the UK, with more workers than the agricultural and clothing industries combined. The National Council for Voluntary Organisations (NCVO) supports voluntary groups, ranging from large national organisations to a single centre working in one community. Religious believers have founded thousands of these organisations, and many are linked with the vihara, church, mandir, mosque, synagogue or gurdwara. Thousands of other voluntary organisations have no link with religion.

Voluntary workers give invaluable **service** to society as they help with an enormous range of activities. These include:

- cleaning up the environment or campaigning for measures to prevent climate change; for example, Friends of the Earth
- social and caring work; for example, the Samaritans
- running or assisting with youth groups and sports teams
- working for political change via pressure groups
- campaigning for better conditions for others via groups, such as Amnesty International
- charity work; for example, Muslim Aid, Christian Aid
- sharing interests, skills or hobbies with others; for example, voluntary work in care homes.

Key terms
Voluntary work: unpaid work, done willingly without expectation of a reward.

Voluntary organisation: an organisation that runs through voluntary contributions or voluntary labour.

Service: the work done by one person or group that benefits another. An act of help or assistance.

Sewa (Seva): selfless service: often refers to voluntary work or work offered to God (Hinduism, Sikhism).

Research activity
Using the internet or a library, find out about Chad Varah and the Samaritans. Make notes on your findings.

Religious attitudes to helping others

Hindus and Sikhs regard service as a duty. They believe that doing **sewa** is to worship God and to work for eternal happiness. The best sort is sewa undertaken without the expectation of any reward, although if done in the right spirit, it will gain merit and produce positive karma. Buddhists also believe that service should be undertaken with the right motive, that is, without selfish intent. Hindus believe that serving people is serving God.

> **Beliefs and teachings**
>
> That gift which is given out of duty, at the proper time and place, to a worthy person, and without expectation or return, is considered to be charity in the mode of goodness.
>
> *Bhagvad Gita 17:20*

AQA Examiner's tip
Make sure that you know the teachings of the religion(s) you are studying about helping those in need.

The Guru Granth Sahib encourages Sikhs to perform sewa and this is often done by work within the gurdwaras. Providing free food in the kitchen (langar), washing dishes and cleaning the floors are all ways that sewa is undertaken. Many also do unpaid work in the community in hospitals, senior citizens homes and community centres.

Christians are taught in the Parable of the Sheep and Goats in the Bible that whenever they help a person in need they are helping Jesus.

> **Beliefs and teachings**
>
> What you did for one of the least of these brothers of mine, you did for me.
>
> *Matthew 25:40*

Muslims believe that Allah expects them to be charitable:

> **Beliefs and teachings**
>
> He who eats and drinks while his brother goes hungry, is not one of us.
>
> *Hadith*

Jews are asked not only to serve their own people but also to help their enemies if they are in need.

> **Beliefs and teachings**
>
> If you see the donkey of someone who hates you fallen down under its load, do not leave it there; be sure you help him with it.
>
> *Exodus 23:5*

Activities

1. Describe some of the types of activities that volunteers undertake in Britain.

2. Explain religious attitudes towards serving others.

3. 'Treat others as you wish to be treated is the best way to live your life.' Do you agree? Give reasons for your answer, showing that you have thought about more than one point of view. Refer to religious arguments in your answer.

Discussion activity

With a partner, in a small group or as a class, discuss whether you agree with the following statement:

'You cannot be called a good citizen unless you do voluntary work.'

Make notes on the opinions given.

Summary

You should now be able to describe some of the types of work volunteers do in Britain, and explain religious attitudes towards serving others.

3.9 The work of religious voluntary organisations

Objectives
Investigate the work done by religious voluntary organisations.

Religious teachings about serving others

The major religions teach that it is important to serve others and this can be done through charity work.

Inspired and motivated by their religious faith, many believers help a **religious voluntary organisation**. This may be done by:

- raising money; for example, organising or helping at a fund-raising event
- giving money
- working as a volunteer
- publicising the work of the charity.

Key terms
Religious voluntary organisation: a religious organisation that operates through voluntary contributions or voluntary labour.

A *Many religious charities have projects in Africa*

Beliefs and teachings

Buddhism 'The greatest quality is seeking to serve others.'
Atisha, Buddhist teacher

Christianity 'So in everything, do to others what you would have them do to you.'
Matthew 7:12

Hinduism 'That gift which is given out of duty, at the proper time and place, to a worthy person, and without expectation of return, is considered to be charity in the mode of goodness.'
Bhagavad Gita 17.20

Islam 'And whoso does good works, whether male or female, and he (or she) is a believer, such will enter paradise.'
Qur'an 4:124

Judaism 'Do not seek revenge or bear a grudge against one of your people, but love your neighbour as yourself.'
Leviticus 19:18

Sikhism 'Compassion-mercy and religion are the support of the entire world.'
Japji Sahib

Case studies

Rokpa
The Tibetan word for 'to help/serve', is 'rokpa'. This is the name of an international Buddhist charity that has its headquarters in Zurich, Switzerland. Rokpa has offices in 18 countries, although it focuses mainly on helping Tibetan refugees, and establishes medical clinics and traditional schools for Tibetan learning and medicine. It sees its function as re-establishing monasteries and preserving the culture of Tibet. Rokpa also helps to feed orphans and the homeless in different parts of Europe.

Tear Fund
Tear Fund's 10-year vision is to encourage 100,000 churches to help 50 million people, so that they are set free from physical and spiritual poverty. Working in 64 countries with other church organisations, Tear Fund has, for example, schemes to introduce drought-resistant crops and

prevent flooding. Many people throughout the world suffer from HIV, unfair trade laws, the effects of climate change and from drinking unclean water. By offering resources to the local churches, Tear Fund hopes that local Christian people will be able to make a positive difference in their communities. Internationally, Tear Fund campaigns for trade justice so that it is easier for the poor to make a living.

Bochasanwasi Shri Akshar Purushottam Swaminarayan Sanstha (BAPS)

Set up in 1977, this is the largest Hindu charity in Britain. It provides help to maintain the Swaminarayan Hindu Mandir in London and money to provide free education in India. Aid is also given to assist the victims of natural disasters; for example, food parcels were sent to Gujarat in India after recent severe flooding in the region. BAPS campaigns against harmful addictions, and organises cultural festivals for those interested in Hinduism.

Muslim Aid

Muslim Aid was set up in 1985 because of famine in Africa. Since then the organisation has expanded to work in over 70 different countries. Initially, its aim was to respond to natural disasters and emergencies but now the focus has been widened to try to help the poor of the less economically developed countries (LEDCs). The organisation helps by providing healthcare, education and skills training, and clean water, and assists people to set up projects that generate an income.

Jewish Care

Jewish Care provides help for Jews living mainly in South East England and London. It employs over 1,000 staff and has around 2,500 volunteer workers. The organisation's aim is to support the elderly and vulnerable members of the Jewish community. It runs community centres to enable Jews to socialise and learn news skills while promoting Jewish culture and traditional Jewish values. The community centres offer day care to those suffering from ill health and they welcome about 7,000 clients each week.

Guru Nanak Nishkam Sewak Jatha (Birmingham) UK

Formed by Baba Puran Singh in the 1970s, this Sikh voluntary organisation works in the UK, Africa and India. Its headquarters are in Birmingham and it has gurdwaras in Leeds and London. Its main work in the UK concerns the provision of prayer services, teaching the scriptures and educational visits for teachers and students. In India and the Punjab, the organisation helps with the restoration or construction of sacred Sikh shrines. In Kenya it is developing hostels, sports facilities and workshops for young people.

Summary

You should now be able to describe the work of a religious voluntary organisation, and be familiar with religious teachings that help to explain why believers support charities.

Extension activity

Using the internet or a library, investigate the case studies further and make notes on your findings.

AQA Examiner's tip

Ensure that you can describe the work of at least one religious voluntary organisation.

links

For more on voluntary work and service to others, see pages 66–67.

Discussion activity

With a partner, in a small group or as a class, discuss whether you agree with the following statement:

'Everyone should do voluntary work, not just religious believers.'

Make notes on the opinions given and the reasons for them.

Activities

1. Give a religious teaching that encourages support for voluntary organisations.

2. Describe the work of a religious voluntary organisation.

3. Give three ways believers can help voluntary organisations.

4. 'Religious believers should help at a charity fund-raising event at least twice a year.' What do you think? Explain your opinion.

3.10 Unemployment and the value of work

■ Unemployment

When businesses are doing well and expanding, then levels of **unemployment** fall. When there is a recession, the rate rises. The unemployed may receive help from the government, including jobseeker's allowance, income support and help with housing costs. Those who have disabilities may be eligible for incapacity benefit or severe disability allowance. Support for the unemployed is funded out of taxes paid by those in work.

The reasons why a person is unemployed include:

- insufficient skills and qualifications
- inappropriate skills in the area in which they live
- lack of experience
- competing with younger workers with more up-to-date skills
- having a disability that makes it difficult to find suitable employment
- poor motivation and laziness
- redundancy in a time of recession.

Unemployment can result in:

- people being unable to meet their financial obligations, and so getting into debt
- mortgages being unpaid and houses being repossessed, leaving families homeless
- stress in the home and strains on relationships
- loss of dignity, self-respect and boredom
- businesses in an area suffering, resulting in more unemployment if trade is weak and workers are laid off.

■ The value of work

All the religions believe in the value of work, but also in the need to give proper attention to worship and prayer. This is normally achieved by the observance of holy days and festivals.

Religious teachings

Buddhists believe in employment and right livelihood as it helps a person develop skills and contribute positively to society. Buddhists do not have a specific day of worship but in Buddhist countries there are public holidays on festival days, allowing the celebration, for example, of Wesak or Songkran.

Christians believe that work is important and in the Bible St Paul suggests a very tough approach to those who are lazy:

> **Beliefs and teachings**
>
> If a man will not work, he shall not eat.
>
> *2 Thessalonians* 3:10

Objectives

Investigate help given to the unemployed.

Examine reasons for unemployment and the effect on the unemployed.

Know religious attitudes to work and holy day issues.

Key terms

Unemployment: the state of being without a job, especially involuntarily.

Research activity

Help for the unemployed

Using the internet or a library, find out more about help for the unemployed. Record your findings.

A *Some communities and religious believers provide food for the unemployed*

∞ links

Remind yourself about the importance of work and the various religions' attitudes to it by re-reading pages 52–53.

However, Sunday is regarded as the day of rest and many Christians have campaigned to keep Sunday special. They believe that Sunday should be a day for worship or a day spent with family and friends, rather than work.

In the past, the 'caste' system affected the work done by Hindus. The 'Brahmins' were the priests and teachers, the 'Kshatriyas' the warriors and rulers, the 'Vaisyas' the merchants, farmers and artisans, the 'Sudra varna' labourers, and the 'Untouchables' did the unpleasant jobs. Today, caste barriers have largely broken down in the large cities. Being employed is important in Hinduism:

Beliefs and teachings

Perform your prescribed duty, for action is better than inaction. A man cannot even maintain his physical body without work.

Bhagavad Gita 3:8

B Buddhists, Muslims and Sikhs are not allowed to work in breweries

In India there are public holidays for festivals like Diwali and Holi, but this does not happen in Britain, making it difficult for Hindu workers to join in with the celebrations.

Islam discourages everyone from remaining unemployed unless there is good reason.

Beliefs and teachings

No one eats better food than that which they have earned by their own labours.

Hadith

Friday is the Muslim holy day. It is, however, a working day in this country and special festivals like Eid occur on workdays.

Jews believe that God ordained work (Genesis 3) and so it is important to seek employment. It is not appropriate, however, to work on Shabbat and holy days. There are 39 forbidden acts of work for the Shabbat, including sowing, ploughing, reaping, baking, weaving and building.

Sikhs believe in the importance of employment in order to gain an income.

Beliefs and teachings

The farmers love to work their farms; they plough and work the fields, so that their sons and daughters may eat.

Guru Granth Sahib 166

Sikhs do not have a specified holy day, but in Britain they usually go to the gurdwara on Sundays, which means that work from Monday to Friday is not a problem for most Sikhs.

Summary

You should now be able to explain the problems of unemployment and religious attitudes to employment and work on holy days.

AQA Examiner's tip

Make certain that you know the teaching of at least one religion about the value of employment and the observance of holy days, and ensure you use the information gained from your research in answers to question about work.

Discussion activity

With a partner, in a small group or as a class, discuss whether you agree with St Paul's attitude that a person who refuses to work should not be given food. Make notes on the opinions given and the reasons for them.

Activities

1. Give reasons why people are unemployed, and explain the problems associated with unemployment.

2. Explain the religious attitudes regarding the value of work.

3. 'If a person is out of work, they should take any job.' What do you think? Explain your opinion.

Assessment guidance

3

Religion and work – summary

For the examination you should now be able to:

- ✔ explain religious attitudes and teachings about the purpose and importance of work
- ✔ give an account of the case study of someone who believes they have a vocation
- ✔ evaluate why some jobs are seen as unacceptable by religious believers
- ✔ explain the rights and responsibilities of employers and employees and religious attitudes towards them
- ✔ explain and evaluate religious attitudes towards business and enterprise, different professions, the economy and taxation, holy day issues, voluntary work and unemployment
- ✔ explain the importance of health and safety and fair wages
- ✔ outline the work and evaluate the importance of trade unions
- ✔ describe and explain different types of voluntary work and service undertaken by religious and non-religious organisations.

Sample answer

1 Write an answer to the following exam question:

'Work is a good thing.'

Do you agree? Give reasons for your answer, showing that you have thought about more than one point of view. Refer to religious arguments in your answer.

(6 marks)

2 Read the following sample answer.

> Work is good because it is God's intention for people to work. Adam was told as he was thrown out of the Garden of Eden that he would have to earn his living 'by the sweat of his brow'. Work is constructive as it enables the economy to work. Without it, there would nothing to buy, no food, no clothes, nothing and it stops people from being bored. People improve their skills and this brings self-respect and he or she is able to fulfil their vocation in life.
>
> On the other hand, too much work is not good as we all need rest and leisure. The Bible says that we should keep the Sabbath day holy and people need time to worship God and relax with their families. Also, some jobs are not good but are destructive, for example, making illegal drugs or pornographic videos.
>
> In my opinion work is good if it is in balance with the rest of our lives as we are able to earn money but too much work and some jobs are not good.

3 With a partner, discuss the sample answer. Do you think that there are other things that the student could have included in the answer?

4 What mark (out of 6) would you give this answer? (Look at the mark scheme in the Introduction on page 7 (AO2) before you attempt this). What are the reasons for the mark you have given?

AQA Examination-style questions

1 Look at the photograph and answer the following questions.

    (a) What is meant by 'sewa'? *(1 mark)*

    (b) Outline the work of a believer who has regarded his or her work as a vocation. *(4 marks)*

    (c) 'Religious believers should encourage people to belong to a team.' What do you think? Explain your opinion. *(3 marks)*

    (d) Give reasons why employers should take health and safety issues very seriously. *(4 marks)*

    (e) 'All religious believers should do some voluntary work to help the community.' Do you agree? Give reasons for your answer, showing that you have thought about more than one point of view. *(6 marks)*

> **AQA Examiner's tip:** Remember that when you are asked if you agree with a statement, you must state what you think as well as the reasons why other people might take a different view. If your answer is one sided, you will only achieve a maximum of 4 marks. If you make no comment about religious belief or practice, you will achieve no more than 3 marks.

4 Religion and the multicultural society

4.1 Multiculturalism

Objectives
Investigate why Britain has become a multicultural society.

A A multicultural class

B Britain has attracted people from all over the world

Why has Britain become a multicultural society?

Britain has attracted people from all over the world for many centuries. The main reasons they have settled here include:

- invasion
- citizenship of a country that was formerly part of the British Empire, allowing them to settle in Britain
- escape from political persecution in their native country
- freedom to practise their religion
- economic opportunities
- encouragement from the UK government.

The history of immigration

Two thousand years ago, the United Kingdom was inhabited by the Celts. Then came the Roman conquest of most of England, and later the Angles, Saxons and the Vikings from Northern Europe invaded and settled. In 1066 the Normans invaded from France and added their way of life to that of the Anglo-Saxons and Celts. A Jewish community joined them. The Jews were expelled in 1290 but were allowed to return under Oliver Cromwell in 1656. Gypsies came to Britain in the 16th century and so did many Huguenots (French Protestant Christians) who were under persecution from Roman Catholics in France.

Key terms
Immigration: moving to another country to live there.
Multicultural: consisting of many cultures, races and religions.

Immigration continued in the 18th century when more French refugees came to Britain during the French Revolution. At the same time, the first Muslims began settling in the port cities of Cardiff, Glasgow, Liverpool and London. These Muslims were mainly sailors on British merchant ships. The largest migration of Muslims has taken place in the last 50 years. Most have come from South Asia, especially Pakistan, India and Bangladesh. As members of the Commonwealth they were attracted by the prospect of employment opportunities and higher wages. They found work in central London, the Midlands, the North and Strathclyde. Many worked in textiles or other manufacturing industries. The 2001 Census showed a total of 1.6 million Muslims in Britain, making it the biggest religious minority group.

Many Africans were brought to Britain as slaves in the 18th and early 19th centuries and stayed here after the abolition of the slave trade. Many Indians, bringing with them Hinduism, and Chinese people came as a result of trade and settled in the major ports. Many Jews came to Britain as a result of persecution in Poland, Ukraine, Russia and Belarus in the 19th century, and there were many Irish settlers who wished to escape the poverty and famine in their homeland.

The First and Second World Wars saw refugees arrive in Britain from many different parts of Europe. For example 250,000 Belgians arrived during the First World War, and many Polish people in the Second World War. In the 1950s and 1960s immigrants came from the Caribbean and other Commonwealth nations as they were invited to help rebuild post-war Britain. Most of Britain's Sikhs have their origins in immigration either from the Punjab in Northwest India, or from East Africa. The number of Buddhists has also increased because of immigration in the 20th century. The London Theravadin Buddhist Society was formed in 1924, and 30 or more years later Zen Buddhists in Britain came from Tibet and its neighbouring countries.

In the 1970s Vietnamese boat people and Asians expelled from Uganda were admitted to the UK. In the 1980s and 1990s the African community expanded and refugees arrived from Eastern Europe, for example from Bosnia and Romania. Recently, the European Union has allowed workers to find employment more easily in member states and thousands of workers from Eastern European countries, such as Poland, have moved to Britain either temporarily or on a permanent basis. There are now more Roman Catholics in Britain than members of the Anglican community, partly because of the Polish immigrants.

This history of immigration shows how Britain has become a **multicultural** society. There is now an estimated minority ethnic population of more than 4 million, which is over 7 per cent of the population.

Extension activity

Use the internet or a library to find out more about the history in Britain of the religion(s) you are studying.

AQA Examiner's tip

Make sure you are able to explain why Britain is a multicultural society.

Discussion activity

With a partner, in a small group or as a class, discuss whether you agree with the idea that there isn't a true British race because centuries of immigration means that all Britons are of mixed blood. Make notes on the opinions given and the reasons for them.

Activities

1. Give reasons why people have immigrated to Britain.
2. Explain the difference immigration has made to the religions in Britain.
3. 'Britain is the most multicultural country in the world.' What do you think? Explain your opinion.

Summary

You should now be able to explain why and how Britain has become a multicultural society.

4.2 Living in a multicultural society

Multicultural Britain

Modern Britain has been greatly influenced by the different ethnic communities that have settled here. Now more than ever before there is greater choice in food, music, fashion, events, media and religion – the result of multiculturalism. Chinese, Italian, Mexican, Greek and Indian restaurants and many more varieties are found in our cities and towns. Supermarkets stock a vast variety of dishes and spices, which were hardly found in Britain fifty years ago. There has never been such a wide selection of foods, some of which meet the requirements of specific religions such as kosher food for Jews and halal meat for Muslims.

Music styles from Africa, the Far East and Caribbean can now be heard in the UK, and the latest fashions in clothes are often based on a unique combination of ethnic styles.

The events in the UK calendar include many additional cultural, social and religious **celebrations**, which reflect the **differences** within society. The Chinese New Year, Yom Kippur, Ramadan, Notting Hill Carnival, Diwali and many more have been added to the traditional Christian festivals.

A Participants wear flamboyant costume at the Notting Hill Carnival as they celebrate multicultural Britain

B Traditional Chinese New Year lion dancing

Objectives

Investigate what it means to live in a multicultural society

Key terms

Celebrations: festivities to mark special occasions or events.

Differences: being different or unlike.

Diversity: differences in customs, religious beliefs or opinion.

Research activity

Using the internet or a library, research what newspapers and magazines are produced in Britain for ethnic minority groups, and record your findings.

There are special television and radio stations for minority groups such as Zee TV (Asian Communities), Alpha Punjabi (Punjabi community), Bollywood 4 U, Star News (Indian Community), Prime TV (Pakistani community), Bangla TV (Bangladeshi Community) and Sirasa TV (Tamil Community), Sunrise Radio, London and a range of newspapers and magazines.

In sport, men and women from minority ethnic groups have enhanced Britain's success in international competitions like the Olympics, the World and European championships and the Commonwealth Games. Key sportspeople from minority ethnic groups have made significant contributions in sports such as athletics, football, cricket and boxing.

Religion in Britain

Britain allows freedom for those who live here to practise whatever religion they wish. In the 2001 Census the main faiths identified, with percentage figures of the total population, were:

- Christianity: 71.6%
- Islam: 2.7%
- Hinduism: 1.5%
- Sikhism: 0.6%
- Judaism: 0.5%
- Buddhism: 0.3%

Religious **diversity** can be found in many different areas of life in Britain. In politics there are now faith-based political parties, such as the Islamic Party of Britain, and there are Muslim and Jewish schools in addition to many Christian schools, run by different denominations such as the Roman Catholic Church, the Anglicans and Methodists.

London (Case study)

London is one of the most cosmopolitan cities in the world. It has attracted residents from countries all over the world and is visited by thousands of international tourists. A survey among children in London showed that over 250 languages are spoken as a first language in Britain's capital. The next most popular languages after English were: Bengali and Silheti, Panjabi, Gujerati and Hindi/Urdu. English was the first language of less than 72 per cent. This makes it difficult for schools to cater for all the different languages and for the students from minority ethnic groups to understand the lessons. While the 2001 Census showed that in England as a whole 87 per cent of the population are white British, in London it was less than 60 per cent, with 3.2 per cent considering themselves to be of mixed race.

In addition to hundreds of churches for many different denominations there are around 40 Hindu temples, 25 Sikh temples and 150 mosques in London. Tower Hamlets has the highest proportion of Muslim residents of any British local authority area.

AQA Examiner's tip

Make sure you are able to explain what it means to live in a multicultural society.

Discussion activity

With a partner, in a small group or as a class, discuss whether you think that all the choice available (food, music, religion, television, celebrations) is an advantage or a disadvantage. Make notes on the opinions given.

Activities

1. Explain what the terms 'ethnic minorities' and 'religious diversity' mean.

2. Give examples of the practical differences of living in a multicultural society.

3. 'Multiculturalism brings a variety of riches.' What do you think? Explain your opinion. You could refer to the London case study in your answer.

Summary

You should now be able to give examples of how residents from ethnic minorities have added to the way of life of people living in Britain.

4.3 Advantages and disadvantages of multiculturalism

Positives and negatives

Living in a multicultural society has both advantages and disadvantages. There is a delicate balance between things working out for the good of everyone and things going wrong. There are, however, many positive features of a society that has a mixture of races, **cultures** and religions. These positives in a society may include:

- a diversity of cultures and lifestyles, which enriches a society and makes life more interesting
- different traditions, customs and ways of celebrating religious festivals
- a wide variety of cuisine
- different sorts of music (for example, reggae, steel band music, hip hop, Latin music, bhangra)
- opportunities for learning about and understanding the way people of other cultures and societies think
- help in overcoming ignorance, arrogance and other forms of prejudice
- a more dynamic economy with more jobs
- access to crucial skills and new ideas
- better public services (for example, many doctors, dentists, nurses, cleaners and care workers are from ethnic minorities).

> **Objectives**
> Investigate the advantages and disadvantages of a multicultural society.

> **Key terms**
> **Culture**: the customs and way of life of a group of people, including religious beliefs.

A A multicultural society offers a wide variety of cuisine

B One advantage of living in a multicultural society is being exposed to different types of music, such as steel band music

Chapter 4 Religion and the multicultural society

Better workforce
Case study

We live in a global economy and many countries and companies are sensitive to discrimination issues, so having a diverse workforce is an advantage. Where competition is great, it helps if someone is of the culture and language of a company's potential customers.

Mike Armstrong, former chairman of AT&T (the world's largest provider of telephone services) said, 'A diverse workforce enhances our creativity and understanding of customers.' (*Organizational Behaviour: Managing People and Organization*, Moorhead and Griffin, 2001) A diverse workforce can help businesses supply a greater variety of solutions to problems in service, sourcing and allocation of resources. The employees are likely to be more creative and have a greater variety of ideas because of their backgrounds, individual talents and experiences, which will assist in meeting customer demands and expectations.

A multicultural society may, however, have negative aspects or potential problems. There may be:

- prejudice and bad behaviour towards people from different ethnic groups
- unrest between different groups
- a tendency to blame immigrants if there is high unemployment or a lack of housing
- communication problems where different languages are spoken
- difficulties for schools trying to teach students of different backgrounds
- problems if one ethnic group suffers greater economic hardship
- a marginalisation or isolation of an ethnic minority group
- difficulties in meeting the requests of different ethnic groups for time off work to celebrate their individual festivals.

There is always a danger that xenophobia (hatred of foreigners) may result if the majority population feels threatened in any way. Also, a minority group may be singled out for persecution if things in the country are not going well, such as happened to the Jews in Nazi Germany and, more recently, to Gypsies in several European countries.

Slavery in Egypt
Case study

Xenophobia is not new. In the Bible, Exodus 1 tells how the Hebrews became a large ethnic group in Egypt. This resulted in the Pharaoh fearing their power. As a result, he made the Hebrews slaves and forced them to build the cities of Pithom and Raamses. He even gave orders that the Egyptian midwives should kill all male Hebrew babies. Moses was saved and eventually led the Hebrews out of slavery, to the land of Canaan.

Summary
You should now be able to explain the benefits of a multicultural society and some of the problems associated with a diverse citizenship.

AQA Examiner's tip
Make sure that you are able to discuss both the advantages and disadvantages of living in a multicultural country.

Discussion activity
With a partner, in a small group or as a class, discuss the risks of having many different ethnic groups and cultures living together in one country. Can religious believers help people live together in peace? Make notes on the opinions given.

Activities
1. Explain the advantages of being a citizen in a multicultural society. Refer to 'Better workforce' case study in your answer.
2. Explain three problems of a living in a diverse community.
3. 'The biggest threat to multiculturalism being a success is prejudice.' Do you agree? Give reasons for your answer, showing that you have thought about more than one point of view.

4.4 Religion and politics

Objectives
Investigate the involvement of religion in politics.

Debate whether religion and politics should mix.

■ Systems of government

In a few countries, religion and **politics** have been so interrelated that the state could be called a 'theocracy'. For example, some Islamic and Jewish societies have regarded only God and his law as sovereign, or supreme in authority. In a pure theocracy, the civic leader is believed to have a direct personal connection with God. For example, Moses ruled the Israelites and was believed to have received the Ten Commandments direct from God on Mount Sinai. The prophet Muhammad ruled the early Muslims and is considered to have received the Law and the Qur'an by divine revelation. Some countries, like Saudi Arabia and Iran, have very strong links between religion and the government. In other countries religion, the government and politics are completely separate.

A Houses of Parliament, London

Key terms
Politics: the activities and affairs involved in managing a government, and the making of decisions that affect others' lives.

■ Believers and politics

Buddhism

Buddhists are very involved in politics in Sri Lanka and the government has retained close ties with the sangha (Buddhist community). In the Jataka (one of the Buddhist scriptures) the Buddha gave ten rules for good government, known as 'Dasa Raja Dharma'. Buddhist monks are not encouraged to be actively engaged in politics.

Christianity

Many British Christians are involved in politics. In 2001 the organisation Christians in Politics was formed to encourage Christian involvement in the Labour, Conservative and Liberal Democrat parties. One of their initiatives has been to hold an annual Westminster Carol Service and to encourage churches to have a Politics Sunday. Some Christians do not think religion and politics mix. Jesus is quoted in the Bible as having said:

Extension activities

1. Using the internet or a library, find out more about different types of government, such as democracy and dictatorship, so that you understand the alternatives to theocracy.

2. Use the internet or a library to find out more about religious believers and their involvement in politics, and record your findings.

> **Beliefs and teachings**
>
> Then give to Caesar what is Caesar's, and to God what is God's.
>
> *Luke* 20:25

Hinduism

Hindus play a prominent role in politics in India, but not in Britain. However, one of the three main areas of interest for the Hindu Forum of Britain (HFB) is public affairs and community consultation. With over 275 member organisations in Britain, more interest is being taken in politics, particularly at local government level.

Islam

Muslims are actively engaged in British politics and the number of Muslim councillors and MPs has increased in recent years. Although those elected are from the main political parties, a specific Muslim

B Should religion and politics mix?

party, the Islamic Party of Britain, has been formed. Muslim political parties rule several countries, such as Iran.

Judaism

Lionel Rothschild was the first Jewish MP, but he had difficulty in taking his seat because he refused to take a Christian oath. In 1858 a compromise was worked out and he was able to swear his oath on the Old Testament. Although Benjamin Disraeli was a Jew by birth, he was a Christian by religion so Britain has not yet had a Jewish Prime Minister. The first Jewish party leader was Michael Howard, who was leader of the Conservative Party from 2003 to 2005.

Sikhism

The Sikh community is generally politically aware and the main political parties try to attract their votes in elections. Some have been involved as councillors and MPs as laws do affect their religious traditions, such as the wearing of turbans.

Should religion and politics mix?

There are arguments for and against mixing religion and politics. Some of these are listed below:

Against

- Politics is a struggle for power; religion is concerned with spiritual things.
- Members of other faiths (or none) may take offence if religion influences politics.
- Political beliefs and religious beliefs may be in conflict; for example, Roman Catholics oppose abortion, but the state does not.
- MPs are expected to vote with their political party. What if this conflicts with their faith?
- It might lead to laws that do not reflect what most people believe.

For

- It is important to have just laws and honest people in government.
- Religious believers feel it is right to influence people on moral issues.
- Some politicians are involved for their own ends; religious believers should think of others first.
- It is important to protect religious freedom.
- Every area of life should be represented in politics, including minority faith groups.
- Politicians need divine guidance.
- Mixing religion and politics might help to stop extremism and terrorism.

Research activity

Use the internet to find out more about how the religion(s) you are studying are involved in politics.

AQA Examiner's tip

Make sure you are able to argue for and against religious involvement in politics.

Discussion activity

Discuss the following statement by Britain's Chief Rabbi, Jonathan Sacks:

'I can't imagine anything worse than rule by religious leaders and I would have nothing to do with it.'

Now make notes on the opinions given here for and against mixing religion and politics, and the reasons for them.

Activities

1. Explain why some people argue that religion and politics should not mix.

2. 'Religion and politics cannot be separated.' What do you think? Explain your opinion.

Summary

You should now be able to discuss whether religion and politics should mix.

4.5 State religion and blasphemy laws

State religion

In the UK the official **state religion** is Christianity, and the Church of England (the Anglican denomination) is the established church in England. For nearly a thousand years the Pope was in charge of Christians in England, but all that changed in 1534. King Henry VIII wanted to end his marriage to Catherine of Aragon, so that he could marry Anne Boleyn. The Pope refused to annul his first marriage and so Henry declared himself the Supreme Head of the Church of England. He was excommunicated by Pope Paul III, but England had become a Protestant country. For a hundred years there was a power struggle between Catholics and Protestants, and then between Anglicans and Presbyterians, but under Charles II the Anglican Church became the established church, as it is today, formally recognised and given a privileged status by the state.

> **Objectives**
>
> Investigate what is meant by 'state religion'.
>
> Find out about blasphemy laws.

> **Key terms**
>
> **State religion**: the official religion of a country.
>
> **Freedom of choice**: the idea that people can choose whatever they wish.
>
> **Blasphemy laws**: the laws that prevent talk or behaviour that insults God or the gods.

A Queen Elizabeth II

The monarch is required to be a member of the Church of England and to not marry a Roman Catholic. Queen Elizabeth II has the titles 'Supreme Governor of the Church of England' and 'Defender of the Faith'. On appointment, the Church of England bishops swear an oath of loyalty:

> *I accept Your Majesty as the sole source of ecclesiastical, spiritual and temporal power.*
>
> www.centreforcitizenship.org/church2.html

The monarch has to approve the appointment of archbishops and bishops, formally open each new session (every five years) of the General Synod (the Church's governing body), and promise in his or her coronation oath to maintain the Church.

The Church of England is also involved in making laws. Twenty-six bishops, including the two archbishops, sit in the House of Lords and are known as the 'Lords Spiritual'. Anglicans also have a civic responsibility in performing state weddings and funerals, acts of remembrance, memorial services and special occasions, such as a coronation.

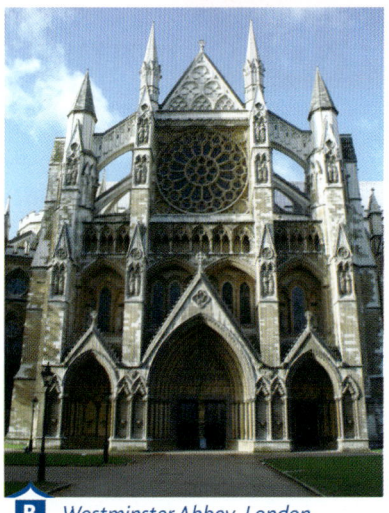

Should the Anglican Church have a privileged position?

Many people see the current situation as a tradition and part of the heritage and culture of Britain. It has worked well, they say, so why change it? Others argue that times have changed and that, as we now live in a multi-faith society, everyone should have **freedom of choice** concerning what faith, if any, to join. For example, the Lords Spiritual could be made up of a variety of Christian denominations and other faiths to reflect the religious make-up of Britain. State occasions also ought to reflect all faiths rather than allowing one Christian denomination to have a special status. The main political parties currently say that they will not disestablish the Church of England until the Church's General Synod requests it.

B Westminster Abbey, London

Blasphemy laws

The current **blasphemy law** is based on decisions made in a court case in 1838, which restricted the law of blasphemy to protecting the 'beliefs of the Church of England'. In 1977, a trial judge defined blasphemous libel as a publication about God, Christ, the Christian religion or the Bible that vilified Christianity and used words which were scurrilous, abusive or offensive. The last person sent to prison for blasphemy was John Gott in 1922, because he compared Jesus to a circus clown.

British Muslims tried to use this law against Salman Rushdie, after he published *The Satanic Verses* in 1988, but discovered that the blasphemy laws only apply to the Church of England. Many Muslims take great offence at insults against the prophet Muhammad and so would like the law extended, and some from other minority faiths would agree.

Others would like to see the law abolished because it is seen as being against freedom of speech (the right to say whatever they want). Many argue that the recent law against incitement to religious hatred in 2006 has superseded the blasphemy law, as it protects **all** religions.

Discussion activity

With a partner, in a small group or as a class, discuss whether you agree with the following statement:

'People should have the freedom of choice to say what they want about religion.'

Make notes on the opinions given and the reasons for them.

AQA Examiner's tip

You need to be aware of the arguments for and against an established church and blasphemy laws.

Activities

1. Explain why the Church of England became the established church in England.
2. Explain why many people think the current law on blasphemy is wrong.
3. 'Having an established church is wrong in a multicultural society.' What do you think? Explain your opinion.

Summary

You should now be able to explain why Britain has a state religion and what the blasphemy law was designed to eliminate.

4.6 Immigration

> *We celebrate the diversity in our country, get strength from the cultures and the races that go to make up Britain today.*
>
> Former Prime Minister, Tony Blair, 2 October 2001

Objectives
Investigate the topic of immigration and why people come to live in Britain.

links
'Immigration' is defined and introduced on pages 74–75. The term 'diversity' is defined on pages 76–77. You can look up both terms in the Glossary at the back of this book.

A People come to Britain from all over the world

Key terms
- **Emigration**: people leaving their home country to go and live in another country.
- **Tolerance**: the permitting of social, cultural and religious differences without protest, discrimination or interference.
- **Respect**: an attitude of consideration and regard for the rights and feelings of others.

Immigration and emigration

During 2007 over 860 immigrants were legally coming to Britain each day, on average. In the preceding 10 years, almost 2.4 million legal immigrants made Britain their home, and 715,000 British citizens moved to other countries. **Emigration** has been mainly to Australia, France and Spain. Australia is popular because it is English speaking and traditionally has been recruiting people with certain skills. France has lower property costs than the UK, which makes it an attractive destination, and Spain has a large population of Britons attracted by the climate.

Most of the new arrivals into Britain were not from EU countries, but 700,000 economic migrants have come from the eight states of Eastern Europe that recently joined the European Union (Estonia, Latvia, Lithuania, Poland, the Czech Republic, Slovakia, Hungary and Slovenia).

Why do people come to Britain?

Economic reasons. Wages in Britain are higher than in many countries, such as the Eastern European countries, Africa or India. The potential to earn more and have a higher standard of living is very attractive. The poorest people in Britain would be among the richest in some countries in Africa.

Research activity
People cannot legally just come and live permanently in Britain. Use the internet or a library to find out about the British Citizenship Test, the fees that have to be paid and the ceremony to celebrate becoming a British Citizen.

Job opportunities. Britain has had a high employment rate and many skills are in great demand. For example, without immigrants the National Health Service would collapse, and the hospitality and construction industries, which have relied heavily on immigrant workers, would suffer.

Tolerance, respect and freedom. Britain has a reputation for tolerance, respect of different cultures and of the right of people to be different. In some countries, religious and minority groups face persecution.

To escape war. Some migrants come to Britain to escape conflict in their homeland.

AQA Examiner's tip

Immigration is a topic that people have very strong views about. Be careful not to show prejudice when you answer questions, and demonstrate in the evaluation questions that you have considered more than one point of view.

Case study

NHS

In the National Health Service in England (2006):

- 38 per cent of all doctors qualified abroad
- 58 per cent of new doctors were not born in Britain
- 40 per cent of dentists came from other countries
- 44,000 nurses came from overseas.

Because immigrants tend to be younger than the average population in Britain, they require less healthcare than those who have lived here all their lives.

Discussion activity

With a partner, in a small group or as a class, discuss what you think religious believers might suggest to help overcome problems of prejudice. Make notes on the suggestions made.

Why does Britain need immigrants?

Essential skills. Immigrants provide skills which Britain needs; for example, in the NHS, public services and the IT industry.

Contribution to the economy. Britain has an aging population. By 2026, pensioners will outnumber children by two million. Most immigrants are young working people, are less likely to need to claim a pension and will contribute to the economy for a longer period.

Motivation. Many immigrants are well motivated and are prepared to do jobs that many native British citizens do not wish to do because they are regarded as demeaning, such as fruit picking and cleaning.

Problems with immigration

Immigration can cause problems in society.

- Some British citizens see new arrivals as a threat; they are worried about loss of jobs.
- Some British citizens are prejudiced against people of different races, languages and religions.
- Planning is required to integrate immigrants into society.
- Racial or religious tension can upset a community.
- Political parties, such as the British National Party, wish to stop all non-white immigration.
- If too many people arrive too quickly, there would not be enough houses, health services would be put under pressure and there would be insufficient school places.

Activities

1. What is the difference between immigrants and emigrants?
2. Give reasons why immigrants wish to come to Britain.
3. Explain three problems that immigration can cause.
4. 'Without immigrants, this country would have real problems.' What do you think? Explain your opinion. Refer to the NHS case study in your answer.

Summary

You should now be able to explain why immigrants come to Britain, and discuss the advantages and disadvantages of immigration.

4.7 Asylum seekers, integration and faith communities

Objectives
Know and understand about asylum seekers, integration and faith communities.

A People come to Britain looking for help

Asylum seekers

Each year thousands of people ask to enter Britain, claiming to be refugees from their homelands. They request asylum, saying they want to live in safety and security. In 2007, 23,430 applications by **asylum seekers** were received by the Home Office, but out of these only 6,540 were successful. The majority of successful applicants came from Afghanistan, Iran, China and Iraq – countries where the human rights record has not been good. Those who are not successful are asked to leave Britain or are deported back to their country of origin. Most religious believers support the giving of asylum to those who are fleeing persecution.

Case study

Should asylum have been granted?

Sometimes it is hard to understand why asylum isn't granted. Emily Dugan reported on such a case in the *Independent* in 2007. Mary, a mother of two from Uganda, was held captive, repeatedly raped and beaten by soldiers because her brother-in-law was a rebel. She managed to escape to England in 2003, but her interview with the Home Office was delayed while she was operated on because of her injuries. The GP did not send a medical report and she was refused entry. Her appeal was heard in 2005, but again she was denied asylum. Left homeless and without money and very scared, she survived on Red Cross food parcels. Will she and others like her ever be granted asylum?

Beliefs and teachings

Buddhism 'The greatest quality is seeking to serve others.'
Atisha, Buddhist teacher

Christianity 'Love your neighbour as yourself.'
Mark 12:31

Hinduism 'Do not do to others what would cause pain if done to you.'
Mahabharata 5:1517

Islam 'And whoso does good works, whether male or female, and he (or she) is a believer, such will enter paradise.'
Qur'an 4:124

Judaism Do not mistreat an alien or oppress him, for you were aliens in Egypt.
Exodus 22:21

Sikhism No one is my enemy, none a stranger and everyone is my friend.
Guru Granth Sahib 1299

Integration or segregation?

It is natural for ethnic minority groups to want to live with people of their own race and faith. **Segregation**, which involves separating people into groups according to their race or religion, however, does not encourage a feeling of belonging to a community. To prevent tension, new residents and existing residents need to **integrate**, to mix with one another and build trust. This can help prevent misunderstanding and gives an opportunity to show tolerance and respect to people of different origins and faiths. The government has encouraged **political correctness (PC)** in order to avoid different groups within society being offended and upset.

Faith communities

In London, immigrants tend to live in neighbourhoods where there are people of their own race and faith, as well as other immigrants and members of the resident population. In time, **faith communities** are established.

The largest British Buddhist community is Soka Gakkai (Value Creation Society) International. It was started in London in the 1960s and now has around 6,000 lay members. It offers Buddhist teaching to the community and campaigns for peace in the world. Together with Tibetan, Zen, Thai, Friends of the Western Buddhist Order and New Kadampa Tradition, the Buddhist community in London is growing and using its influence to spread peace and harmony.

Large Hindu communities in Britain are found in Wembley and Harrow, London. The largest mandir (temple) outside India is found in North West London. The BAPS Shri Swaminarayan Mandir (or Neasden Temple) was opened in 1995. During its construction nearly 3,000 tons of Bulgarian limestone and 2,000 tons of Italian marble were sent to a team of 1,526 sculptors in India. The mandir cost over £12 million and was Europe's first traditional Hindu stone temple. The shrines are opened at set times for worship, and over three million people have visited the temple.

Key terms

Asylum seeker: a person who is seeking to be recognised as a refugee and requests permission to live in safety in another country.

Segregation: the separation of people according to their race or religion.

Integration: different communities starting to live and work together and see each other as equals.

Political correctness (PC): describes language, ideas, policies or behaviour seen as trying to minimise offence to racial, cultural or other identity groups.

Faith community: a group of people belonging to the same religion.

Discussion activity

With a partner, in a small group or as a class, discuss what attitude religious believers should have towards asylum seekers or immigrants. Make notes on the opinions given and the reasons for them.

AQA Examiner's tip

The issue of asylum is very controversial. Make sure you are clear about the arguments for and against letting all asylum seekers settle in Britain.

Activities

1. Why do many people who are seeking asylum wish to come to Britain?
2. Explain what is meant by 'integration into society'.
3. 'Britain has gone 'PC' mad.' What do you think? Explain your opinion.

Summary

You should now be able to explain what asylum seekers are requesting and their reasons for doing so.

You should now know and understand what the terms integration, segregation and political correctness mean.

4.8 Faith communities

■ Faith communities in Britain

Governments recognise the positive role that faith communities can play, and encourage religious believers to help make important decisions in their local areas.

Christianity

Hope 2008 is a recently formed Christian initiative. Its aim is to encourage all Christian denominations to work together to serve the whole community by giving support to non-religious organisations and by taking part in activities to help create a sense of belonging, such as acts of kindness. For example, Christians in South Molton, Devon, cleaned the street signs, collected litter in the parks, delivered plants to people who had recently arrived in the town, made a point of saying thank you to those who provided services, and invited all residents to a free cream tea in the Pannier Market.

Judaism

Some faith groups have a strong influence in certain areas; for example, Jews first settled in the East End of London from Russia, Germany, Spain, Portugal, North Africa and Eastern Europe in particular. Now, many have moved to Golders Green and Stamford Hill. At Stamford Hill there is a Hasidic community of about 20,000 Jews. The Jewish Sabbath is welcomed in by playing Jewish music, and many shops sell specifically kosher food.

Islam

Forty per cent of the total English Muslim population live in London (98% are Sunni Muslims). The most famous mosque is London Central or Regent's Park Mosque with its Islamic Cultural Centre (ICC), where most of the congregation is of Arab descent. The ICC provides many services for the Muslim community, including a Social Services and Health Services Department. Advice is given on topics such as marriage, divorce, health and safety at work, public health advice, halal food and food safety.

Sikhism

Most British Sikhs live in the South East (Greater London area) of England, or the West Midlands. The famous Sri Guru Singh Sabha Southall (SGSSS) Gurdwara is the largest Sikh temple outside India. Costing £17.5 million to build, it was opened in 2003. Recently, a new Sikh School was founded, known as the Khalsa School.

■ Faith projects

Faith groups have started many charities to help alleviate poverty both in Britain and abroad.

Objective

Understand the role and importance of faith communities in Britain and worldwide.

A As part of Hope 2008 local Christians cleaned the signs in their town

links

Faith communities are introduced on pages 86–87 and defined in the Glossary at the back of this book. For Buddhist and Hindu faith communities, see also pages 86–87.

Research activity

Using the internet or a library, research the projects being undertaken by a voluntary organisation supported by the religion(s) you are studying; for example, Tzu Chi, Christian Aid or Red Crescent. Record your findings.

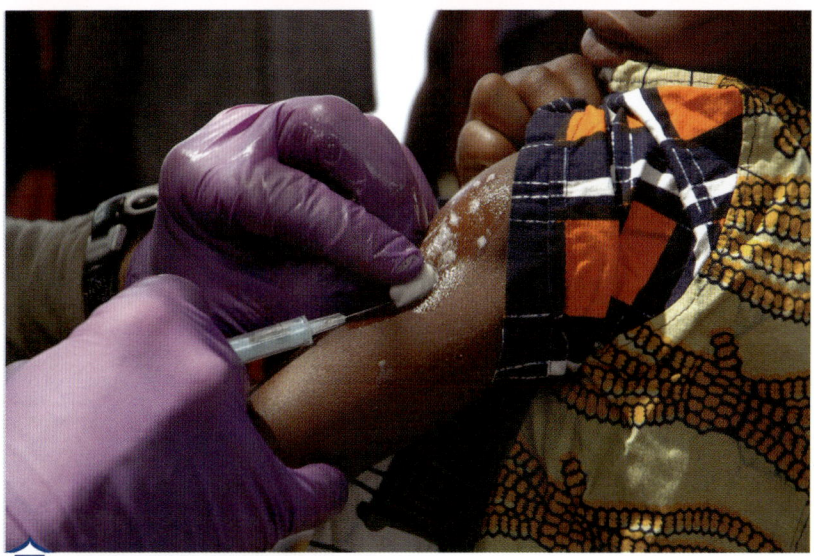

Chapter 4 Religion and the multicultural society

B Vaccinating a child in Africa

C Religious charities provide clean water for a village

Sometimes, different faith communities join together in schemes to benefit their area. Mother and toddler groups, youth groups and various social activities help to bring the community together. These groups working together are called 'interfaith groups'.

Faith groups have also organised conferences to voice their concerns about the environment. For example, Buddhist, Christian, Hindu, Muslim and Jewish leaders met in Assisi, Italy, in 1986 and issued the Assisi Declarations. This was an historic move by religious communities to unite on the major issue of protecting the environment. A subsequent interfaith conference, the Summit on Religions and Conservation, was held in 1995 in Ohito, Japan. Another interfaith conference followed in 2002, at Windsor Castle, England, with major faiths, including Sikhs, participating. The aim of these conferences is to encourage people of faith locally, nationally and internationally to take part in projects to protect the environment and prevent climate change.

Another interfaith group, Religions for Peace, met in Hokkaido, Japan, in July 2008. One hundred religious leaders representing a wide spectrum of religions, including Buddhism, Christianity, Hinduism, Islam and Judaism, called on the G8 (eight richest nations) governments to take action on violent conflict and climate change. In a press release Religions for Peace stated, 'We are united in our call to the G8 to take bold action to address the threats that confront humanity, including the destruction of the environment and climate change, extreme global poverty and deteriorating food security, nuclear arms, terrorism and violent conflict.' (Source: http://www.wcrp.org/news/press/g8-07-03-08)

Religions for Peace was founded in 1970 and in recent years has worked for reconciliation in Iraq, has mediated between the warring groups in Sierra Leone, has set up an international network of religious organisations for women, and has organised a programme to help African children affected by AIDS (the Hope for African Children Initiative).

AQA Examiner's tip

Make sure you are able to describe the work of faith communities and explain what benefit this work is bringing to society.

Discussion activity

With a partner, in a small group or as a class, discuss whether you think the Hope 2008 project is a good idea.

Activities

1. Explain how faith groups help their local communities.

2. Describe the work done by a project run by a faith group.

3. 'People don't take notice of what religious groups say or do.' What do you think? Explain your opinion.

Summary

You should now be able to explain some influences of faith communities locally, nationally and internationally. You should know about and understand some projects run by faith communities.

4.9 Wesak, Christmas and Diwali

Wesak

Wesak is an important **festival** because at this time Buddhists celebrate the birthday of the Buddha. For some Buddhists it marks his death as well. It is also seen as a time to remember the Buddha's enlightenment and it is celebrated at the time of the full moon in May. It is a joyful and colourful festival and homes are cleaned and decorated. During the festival, Buddhists visit the local temple for services, to chant, to pray and to receive teaching. Offerings of food, candles and flowers are given to the monks. It is the tradition in Thailand to make special Wesak lanterns out of paper and wood, and caged birds are released. In some Buddhist traditions 'Bathing the Buddha' takes place. Water is poured over the Buddha, reminding believers of the need to purify the mind from greed, hatred and ignorance. Vegetarian food is sometimes eaten in the temples. Chinese Buddhists include traditional dancing dragons in their celebrations. Gifts are often given and visits made to orphanages and homes for the elderly. Some may give blood to the hospitals or take part in some other charitable act.

Christmas

Christmas is the Christian season that celebrates the birth of Jesus. In Britain, Christmas Day is on 25 December, although the actual day of the birth of Jesus is not known. There are 12 days of the Christmas season, starting on 25 December and continuing until 5 January. Some Christian denominations, such as the Armenian Apostolic Church, celebrate Christmas on 6 January and others, such as Jehovah Witnesses, do not celebrate it at all. There are many different worldwide **customs** but in Britain Christians and non-Christians exchange cards, and children look forward to the secret arrival of Father Christmas with presents during the night of 24 December. Shops, streets and homes are decorated with Christmas lights, trees,

> **Objectives**
>
> Know and understand the customs and celebrations of Wesak, Christmas and Diwali, and how they bring religion into the community.

A *Little Buddha statue decorated at Wesak*

B *The nativity scene is often shown on church stained glass windows*

> **Key terms**
>
> **Festival:** a religious celebration.
>
> **Custom:** accepted or habitual practice, usually of long standing.

holly and other decorations, and families try to get together for the Christmas season. Food such as mince pies, Christmas cake, Christmas pudding and roast turkey is eaten, and many parties take place.

Christians see Christmas as a time for promoting peace and goodwill and for giving to charity. They display nativity scenes in their homes and Christmas songs, called carols, are sung. Special celebration services are held, such as Midnight Mass on Christmas Eve, and often on a Sunday near to Christmas, or during the Christmas morning services, children act out the Christmas story.

Diwali (Divali)

This festival as celebrated by Hindus, Jains and Sikhs as the Festival of Light. The lights or lamps are a symbol of the victory of good over evil. Hindus celebrate with firecrackers, fireworks, lights and flowers, and by the giving and receiving sweets and worship. There are various local customs in India but Lakshmi, the goddess of wealth, is thanked and people pray that they will have a good year.

For Sikhs, Diwali symbolises their struggle for freedom. It also reminds them of the story of the release from prison of Guru Hargobind.

At Diwali in Britain, Hindus and Sikhs clean and decorate their homes with lamps and candles. Sweets, such as 'laddoo' and 'barfi', are given and many people exchange gifts through the post with relatives in India. Many non-Hindus and Sikhs also celebrate this festival, and Leicester has one of the biggest celebrations outside India.

C Diwali – Festival of Light

Extension activity

Use the library or the internet to find out more about Wesak, Christmas and Diwali customs, and how they bring people together.

AQA Examiner's tip

Maximise your choice in the exam by knowing about each of the festivals, even if they are celebrated by a religion you are not specifically studying.

Discussion activity

With a partner, in a small group or as a class, discuss whether you agree with the following statement: 'Festivals are just an excuse for religious believers to have a good time.' Make notes on the opinions given.

Activities

1. Describe and explain the customs and celebrations of Wesak, Christmas or Diwali.

2. How do these festivals help to bring communities together?

3. 'Wesak and Diwali should be national public holidays, just like Christmas.' What do you think? Explain your opinion.

Summary

You should now be able to describe the customs and celebrations of at least one of the three festivals, and explain how they help to bring people together and introduce religion into the community.

4.10 Eid-ul-Fitr, Pesach and Baisakhi

Eid-ul-Fitr

Eid-ul-Fitr is the festival at the end of Ramadan, the month of fasting. Muslims celebrate the end of the fasting and give thanks to Allah for the help and strength that enabled them to practise self-control. The celebrations begin at the time the new moon is seen in the sky. New or best clothes are worn, and homes are decorated. Often, stalls decorated with, for example, balloons line the pavements and Eid cards are sent to friends and family. Children receive presents and money is given to the mosque and to those in need (Zakah).

A special meal is eaten during the daytime and religious services are held out-of-doors, as well as in the mosques. The imam gives a speech (bayan), during which he usually encourages Muslims to end any quarrels they have. Following the congregational prayer, the imam declares Eid-ul-Fitr and worshippers greet and hug each other in a spirit of peace and love. People process through the streets and families visit their relatives and friends. In Britain, Eid-ul-Fitr is not a national public holiday but in areas of the country with large numbers of Muslims, schools and businesses often allow the Muslim community to have the day off to celebrate.

Pesach or Passover

Pesach is the Jewish festival that celebrates how God saved the Hebrews when they were slaves in Egypt. All the first-born sons of the Egyptians were killed during the night of the Tenth Plague, when the angel of death passed over the land. This resulted in Pharaoh allowing

B Table set for the Pesach meal

> **Objectives**
> Know and understand the customs and celebrations of Eid-ul-Fitr, Pesach and Baisakhi, and how they bring religion into the community.

A Eid begins at new moon

> **Key terms**
> **Eid-ul-Fitr**: festival to mark the end of the fasting of Ramadan.
> **Pesach**: festival celebrating the exodus of the Israelites from Egypt.
> **Baisakhi**: festival celebrating the formation of the Sikh khalsa.

> **Research activity**
> 1 Using the internet or a library, find out the four questions that are asked during the Seder meal and record your findings.

the Israelites to leave slavery. They left in such a hurry that they could not allow the bread to rise, so Passover is celebrated for one day and this is followed by the Feast of Unleavened Bread for seven days. Instead of leavened bread, unleavened bread (matzah) is eaten and on the first night Jews eat the Passover Seder meal. The finest china and silverware is used and, during the meal, the story of the exodus from Egypt is retold using the Haggadah (special account with questions). Four cups of wine are drunk and each of the seven items on the seder plate are symbolic of the exodus story. Three loaves of matzah bread remind them of the slavery; salt water reminds them of the tears of the slaves; charoset (mixture of almonds, apples, cinnamon and wine) represents the mud they had to turn into bricks; carpas (often parsley or lettuce) dipped in salt water reminds them of the misery of slavery and the tears the slaves wept before they were free; a roasted shank bone represents the sacrificed lamb and a roasted egg recalls the sacrifice in the temple for the Passover.

Baisakhi (Vaisakhi)

Baisakhi is the Sikh New Year festival and the anniversary of the founding of the Khalsa (the Sikh community) in 1699, by Guru Gobind Singh. Sikhs celebrate receiving a clear identity and code of conduct to live by. The community celebrations begin early as worshippers with flowers and offerings proceed to the gurdwaras before dawn. Parades take place and a few days later in Manhattan, New York, for example, Sikhs perform seva (selfless service) by giving out free food or helping people by doing jobs that need to be done. To the people of Nepal and Indians of Kerala, Tamilnadu and West Bengal, it is a day to celebrate the New Year, and in many northern Indian states it is a traditional harvest festival celebration.

C Sikh Khanda (doubled-edged sword): a symbol of Sikhism

Research activity

2. Use the internet or library to research the story of the Panj Piare and the setting up of the Khalsa.

AQA Examiner's tip

Knowing the origins and purpose of the festivals is useful background information to help you understand the impact of the celebrations on the community.

Discussion activity

With a partner, in a small group or as a class, discuss whether you agree with the following statement:

'Festivals are more for children than adults.'

Make notes on the opinions given.

Activities

1. Describe and explain the customs and celebrations of one of the following festivals, and how they bring people together: Eid-ul-Fitr, Pesach, Baisakhi.

2. Give three reasons why people celebrate festivals.

3. 'People spend too much time and money on festivals.' What do you think? Explain your opinion.

Summary

You should now be able to describe the customs and celebrations of at least one of the three festivals, and explain how they help to bring people together and introduce religion into the community.

Assessment guidance

4

Religion and the multicultural society – summary

For the examination you should now be able to:

✔ explain the concepts of multiculturalism, tolerance, respect, diversity and political correctness

✔ discuss whether religion should be involved in politics

✔ explain the advantages and disadvantages of living in a multicultural society

✔ discuss whether Britain should have a state religion or blasphemy laws

✔ give arguments for and against immigration

✔ explain why some people seek asylum

✔ use key teachings to show why religious believers might support asylum seekers and immigration

✔ explain the influence of faith communities

✔ explain the customs and celebrations of key religious festivals, and their importance.

Sample answer

1 Write an answer to the following exam question.

'People should stay in their own country, not immigrate to Britain.'

Do you agree? Give reasons for your answer, showing that you have thought about more than one point of view.

(6 marks)

2 Now read the following sample answer.

> It would be impossible for Britain to cope with everyone coming to this country. The UK is a small island and we have a lot of people here already so immigration should be limited. People in their own country have the benefit of being with their own family and their own customs and religious beliefs.
>
> However, Christians believe that nationality shouldn't matter and that we should not be prejudiced against people from other countries. 'There is neither Jew nor Greek, slave nor free, male nor female, for you are all one in Christ Jesus.' Galatians 3:28. Britain needs doctors, nurses and dentists or our health service would collapse and what about people who are being persecuted in their own land. Don't we have a duty to show compassion like that Good Samaritan did to the injured Jew?

3 With a partner, discuss the sample answer. Do you think that there are other things that the student could have included in the answer?

4 What mark (out of 6) would you give this answer? (Look at the mark scheme in the Introduction on page 7 (AO2) before you attempt this.) What are the reasons for the mark you have given?

AQA Examination-style questions

1 Look at the photograph and answer the following questions.

(a) Explain briefly, using an example, what tolerance means? *(2 marks)*

(b) Explain two reasons why asylum seekers might be allowed into Britain. *(4 marks)*

(c) 'Britain's blasphemy laws should be extended to cover all religions.' What do you think? Explain your opinion. *(3 marks)*

(d) Describe briefly one project run by a faith community. *(3 marks)*

(e) 'Young people should be taught more about religious customs and festivals.' Do you agree? Give reasons for your answer, showing that you have thought about more than one point of view. *(6 marks)*

> **AQA Examiner's tip**
> Remember that when you are asked if you agree with a statement, you must show what you think and the reasons why other people might take a different view. If your answer is one sided, you will only achieve a maximum of 4 marks. If you make no comment about religious belief or practice, you will achieve no more than 3 marks.

5 Religion and identity

5.1 Who am I?

What does it mean to be human?

Humans have a **physical dimension**. Dictionary definitions of 'human' may consist of something similar to the following: 'Humans are bipedal primates belonging to the mammalian species Homo sapiens in the family of Hominidae, characterised by superior intelligence, language and being able to stand erect.'

Unlike other animals, humans also have a **spiritual dimension**, as recognised by Plato:

> *The noblest of all studies is the study of what man should be and of what life he should live.*
>
> Plato

Although it is an important issue, sometimes we make fun of the question of what it means to be human, as in the early 19th century nursery rhyme:

> *What are little boys made of?*
> *What are little boys made of?*
> *Frogs and snails and puppy dogs' tails,*
> *That's what little boys are made of.*
>
> *What are little girls made of?*
> *What are little girls made of?*
> *Sugar and spice and all that's nice,*
> *That's what little girls are made of.*
>
> Anon

A What does it mean to be human?

Objectives
Introduce the topic of what it means to be human.

Key terms
Physical dimension: that which can be experienced by the five senses and the physical body.

Spiritual dimension: relates to the soul or spirit in contrast to material or physical things.

AQA Examiner's tip
Make sure you understand what is meant by the 'physical' and 'spiritual dimensions'.

Discussion activity
With a partner, in a small group or as a whole class discuss what the following quotation means:

'Every human being is intended to have a character of his own; to be what no other is, and to do what no other can do.' William Ellery Channing (1780–1842)

Make notes on the opinions given.

Who am I? What am I?

These are questions that humans have been seeking to answer for thousands of years. Professor C E Joad, an atheist, said:

> *Man is nothing but*
> *Fat enough for seven bars of soap*
> *Iron enough for one medium sized nail*
> *Sugar enough for 7 cups of tea*
> *Lime enough to whitewash a chicken coop*
> *Phosphorous enough to tip 2,200 matches*
> *Magnesium enough for one dose of salts*
> *Potash enough to explode one toy crane*
> *Sulphur enough to rid one dog of fleas.*
>
> *Professor C E Joad*

Is this all human beings are made of, dissolved in some water?

Case study

A human being

There is no startling new element, so at first sight it could be said that humans are not very remarkable in their make-up. But in the body all the ingredients are combined in so many ways that people are made up of thousands of complex chemical compounds. The most abundant substances after water are proteins, which make up 10–20 per cent of the body. Then come inorganic salts, lipids, carbohydrates and nucleic acids. Scientists say that humans are made up of millions and millions of tiny cells of more than 100 different types. Each type is designed to carry out a specific function and also enable the body to reproduce and replace dead cells, so enabling the continuity of human life. Did you know that your heart is beating at a rate of 60 to 70 times per minute? That's around 93,000 times per day, 655,000 times per week, 34,000,000 times per year and 2.4 billion times in an average lifetime. At the same time the liver is detoxifying your blood, the brain is receiving thousands of bits of information and the body is using and producing energy. The human brain is so complex that it contains roughly 100 billion neurons, linked with up to 10,000 connections each. It is capable of abstract reasoning, understanding language, examining thoughts and feelings, problem solving and emotion.

Clearly, the body is more than just a jumble of chemicals; it is a highly organised, marvellously integrated living organism. The human skeleton consists of over 206 fused or individual bones. Ligaments, tendons, muscles and cartilage enable the bones to move or act as a support or protection for all the body's organs.

Every person is unique; there is no one else in the whole world just like you! Even our fingerprints are different, but some people say that we are just advanced animals. What does it mean to be human? Biologically, humans are much like other living organisms carrying the same kind of genetic information system. Have humans simply evolved from monkeys and apes?

Is there more to human beings than just the physical body and the mind? Christians, Hindus, Muslims, Jews and Sikhs say that humans have a soul, which lives on after a person dies.

Activities

1. Explain the physical make-up of humans.

2. 'What are we – just skin and bones?' What do you think? Explain your opinion.

Summary

You should now be able to explain some of the things that make up a human being's physical dimension and how the spiritual dimension of a human might be different.

links

You can find out more about the soul on pages 100–101.

5.2 The value and importance of human life

Case study: Bicentennial Man

In this film, robot Andrew Martin was designed to do housekeeping and maintenance duties, but he seems to have human characteristics, such as emotions. He develops creativity and has surgery to transform him from robot to android. Eventually, he is granted his freedom and becomes human enough to fall in love. He requests to be recognised as human so that he can be legally married, but his request is rejected because, as long as he is immortal, he cannot be human. During the next 100 years, he turns himself into a prosthetic human and begins to age. On his death bed, aged 200 years, the World Congress recognises him as the oldest human being in history.

Objectives

Know and understand religious views about the origins of human life, and what it means to be human.

Extension activity

Watch the Robin Williams film *Bicentennial Man* and discuss the issues raised about humanity. What does it mean to be human?

The value and origins of human life

With the exception of Buddhism, religions teach that **personhood** is special as it is a gift of God. The ability to reason is unique to human beings who have managed to do such things as split the atom and understand genetic engineering. Religions teach that humans are valuable and precious, and they believe in the sanctity of life. But where does human life come from?

Buddhism

Buddhists believe that human rebirth is very rare and precious. One Buddhist scripture compares the chances of being reborn as a human to the likelihood of a blind turtle surfacing from the depths of the ocean once in 100 years, and putting its head straight through the hole in a wooden cattle yoke floating on the sea.

One Buddhist story about human origins suggests that a long time ago there were supernatural beings (devas), shining in their own light, who could move through the air without requiring nourishment. Gradually, these creatures acquired a taste for food and this resulted in a change of appearance and shorter lives. The sexes evolved and greed, theft and violence became common. The people formed governments and elected a king to rule them. Some of kings of India at the time of the Buddha claimed to be descendants of this king, Mahasammata.

A What can compare to new life?

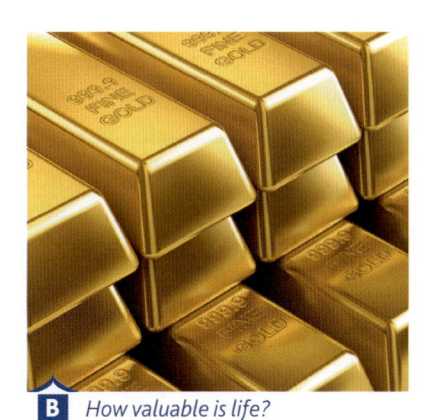

B How valuable is life?

Christianity and Judaism

Christians and Jews believe that God created human beings and made them special and unique among creation.

Beliefs and teachings

So God created man in his own image, in the image of God he created him; male and female he created them.

Genesis 1:27

Key terms

Personhood: the state or condition of being a person, especially having those qualities that confer distinct individuality and the ability to reason.

Christians believe that God is involved in the creation of every human life, and so every child and every person matters.

> **Beliefs and teachings**
>
> For you created my inmost being;
> you knit me together in my mother's womb.
> I praise you because I am fearfully and wonderfully made.
>
> *Psalms 139 13–14*

The Psalmist David puts into context the importance of humans to God.

> **Beliefs and teachings**
>
> What is man that you are mindful of him,
> the son of man that you care for him?
> You made him a little lower than the heavenly beings
> and crowned him with glory and honour.
>
> *Psalms 8 4–5*

Hinduism

In Hinduism there are many stories about the origins of human beings. The Riga Veda tells of the god's sacrifice of the divine primeval form of man, and how the parts of this first being became the various living creatures, including humans. Another Hindu story tells how Brahma created Svayambhuva Manu and a woman called Satarupa, and their sons and daughters spread and inhabited the world.

Islam

The Qur'an teaches that Allah created human beings, giving them unique gifts and abilities, including a soul and conscience, knowledge and free will.

> **Beliefs and teachings**
>
> We created man from sounding clay, from mud moulded into shape....
>
> *Qur'an 15:26*

Eve was made to be Adam's mate.

> **Beliefs and teachings**
>
> It is He Who created you from a single person, and made his mate of like nature, in order that he might dwell with her in love.
>
> *Qur'an 7:189*

Sikhism

Sikhs believe all life, including that of humans, comes from God. God made the universe and keeps it in existence. Creation is part of God and is an expression of God's divine Spirit, God's will and command (hukam). For Sikhs, the final aim of life is to reunite with God (mukti), achieved by working hard at developing the positive human qualities that lead a person to become closer to God.

AQA Examiner's tip

This chapter includes religious beliefs, which may be useful in answering many questions in this unit. You should particularly note the beliefs of the religion(s) you are studying.

Discussion activity

With a partner, in a small group or as a whole class discuss how valuable you think life is.

Make notes on the opinions given and the reasons for them.

Activities

1. Explain what is meant by 'personhood'.

2. Explain the origin and value of human life according to the religion(s) you have studied.

3. Human life is God-given. What do you think? Explain your opinion.

Summary

You should now be able to explain religious beliefs about the origin of human life, and its value.

5.3 The spiritual dimension of life

More than body and mind?

Are we more than the physical body and the mind? Religious believers talk about a spiritual side of life which is not bound by the physical world. Religious experiences may give meaning and purpose to life and result in a person joining a faith community. There is no scientific proof to suggest that the spirit or soul exists, but religious believers talk about a spiritual side to our identity. The soul is often defined as the immortal part of humans, and includes a person's inner awareness. There are many religious beliefs about the soul and what happens after the body dies.

Buddhism

Buddhism teaches that everything is impermanent (anatta), and so there is no unchanging and abiding self or soul. Buddhists believe that the false belief in a permanent self causes many of the human emotional, social and political conflicts. Basically, the Buddha taught that 'you' are not an essential, independent body. Buddhists believe that when a person dies, the body and mind disintegrate and that, if the mind is still not enlightened, it will cause the consciousness to bounce back to an unborn child, so continuing the samsara cycle.

Christianity

Christianity teaches that each human being consists of the body, mind and spirit, or soul. The Roman Catholic Catechism says that the soul is 'the innermost aspect of humans, that which is of greatest value in them, that by which they are most especially in God's image: 'soul' signifies the spiritual principle in humans.' When a person dies, most Catholics believe that the soul either goes to purgatory (a place where you atone for your sins), heaven or hell. Most Protestant Christians do not believe in purgatory, but believe that the soul either goes to be with God (heaven) or is banished from God's presence (hell).

Objectives

Investigate beliefs about the spiritual dimension of life.

links

A definition of 'soul' can be found in the Glossary at the back of this book.

A Praying

B The soul never dies

Hinduism

Hindus call the soul the 'atman'. Brahman is described as the 'supreme soul'. Hinduism has many different beliefs about the origin, purpose and fate of the soul, but the Bhagavad Gita says that the atman is part of Brahman and is unchanging, indestructible and is made up of three components: truth or existence; consciousness or knowledge; and form (bliss). At death, the soul does not die but leaves a body and goes (transmigrates) to another body, based on actions done in the person's life ('karma'). Hindus aim to break free of samsara to reach moksha.

Islam

Some Muslims believe that a soul is received on the fortieth day of pregnancy, while others believe it is on the one hundred and twentieth day. If the individual leads a righteous life and follows the five pillars of Islam, the soul grows nearer to Allah. At death, the soul goes to a place of waiting (barzakh) until the day of judgement, when both body and soul are reunited for judgement. Those who deserve a reward will go to paradise, while others will receive the punishment of hell (jahannam). (See Qur'an 66:8, 39:20)

Judaism

> **Beliefs and teachings**
>
> The Lord God formed the man from the dust of the ground and breathed into his nostrils the breath of life, and the man became a living being.
>
> *Genesis 2:7*

This suggests that God made Adam and Eve's physical bodies and breathed his spirit into them. The spirit or soul is believed to be the part of a person's mind, which constitutes physical desire, emotion and thought. It allows individuals to have some awareness of the existence and presence of God.

Sikhism

Sikhs believe that a human's real personality is the soul (atman). The physical body is only a temporary dwelling place for the eternal atman which is a spark from the Eternal Flame, the supreme atman or God.

> **Beliefs and teachings**
>
> O my self, you are an embodiment of God's Light; know your true origin.
>
> *Guru Granth Sahib 441*

The soul journeys through many life forms and being reborn in human form is seen as a special blessing. Humans have the ability to know what is right, giving Sikhs the opportunity to achieve the purpose of life: to find union with God by following the teaching of the gurus.

Discussion activity

With a partner, in a small group or as a whole class discuss whether or not you agree with the idea behind the following Bible quotation – that the spiritual part of a person is more valuable than anything else:

'What can a man give in exchange for his soul?' (Mark 8:37)

AQA Examiner's tip

It is important to know what at least one religion says about the spiritual nature of humans.

Activities

1. Explain what the religion(s) you have studied teaches about the spiritual side of human identity.

2. 'There is no such thing as a soul.' What do you think? Explain your opinion.

Summary

You should now be able to explain religious beliefs about the spiritual nature of human beings.

5.4 Has life got meaning and purpose?

■ Questions about human existence

Throughout the ages, people have asked many big questions about human existence.

What is the **meaning of life**? Why are we here? What is the nature of life? What is the nature of reality? What is the purpose of life? What is an individual's purpose in life?

Such ultimate questions have brought many types of answer. Life goals include:

- reaching one's potential and make a positive difference to the world
- having a family: 'Be fruitful and increase in number.' (Genesis 1:28)
- searching for wisdom, knowledge and understanding; for example, consider the meaning and purpose of life
- doing what is right and leaving the world a better place
- enjoying life by finding happiness and contentment
- gaining power and authority; for example, to rule over others
- obtaining spiritual knowledge or enlightenment; for example, to get close to God.

Some people believe that:

- life is a mystery, so we will never know the answer
- there is no answer because life is a result of random chance.

Science can describe facts about human existence, but the meaning and purpose of life is a question that religions endeavour to answer.

Buddhism

The Buddha taught that the meaning of life is to become enlightened. Life is full of suffering (dukkha) caused by desire and craving, and this can be overcome by following the Noble Eightfold Path. For Theravadin Buddhists, the aim or goal of life is freedom from suffering by escaping to nibbana and ending the repeated cycle of birth, life, death and rebirth. The Mahayana Buddhists' teaching is based less on the individual and more on the possibility of freedom from suffering for all life.

Christianity

Christians believe in a relationship with God in this world continuing after death. This relationship was broken by sin but through Jesus' death and resurrection, the broken relationship with God may be restored. Through repentance for their sins, trust and belief in Jesus, Christians believe that human beings can get close to God once more.

> **Beliefs and teachings**
>
> I (Jesus) am the way and the truth and the life. No one comes to the Father except through me.
>
> *John 14:6*

Objective
Consider the meaning and purpose of life.

Key terms
Meaning of life: the purpose and significance of human existence.

∞ links
Remind yourself of some of the scientific facts about human existence on pages 96–97.

A Happiness

B Christians believe that Christ died for all

According to Christians, the purpose of life is to love God and to love your neighbour (see Mark 12:30–31).

Hinduism

Hindus believe that there are four main aims in life. These are: kama (sensual pleasure); artha (wealth); dharma (righteousness, morality); and moksha. Moksha is the breaking free from the reincarnation cycle and achieving union of the soul (atman) with the supreme spirit, Brahman.

Islam

Many Muslims believe that their purpose is to submit to Allah's will and to worship and glorify Allah. Their duty is to follow the five pillars of Islam: shahadah (profession of faith); salah (pray five times a day); zakah (charity); sawm (fasting during Ramadan); and hajj (pilgrimage); and to spread the message of Islam. This life is a test, determining on judgement day whether a person goes to paradise or to jahannam (hell).

Judaism

Jews believe that God has made a covenant with the Jewish people and that they have been specially chosen to reveal His nature to the world. Their duty is to fear God and keep his commandments (see Ecclesiastes 12:13–14), and believers should:

> **Beliefs and teachings**
>
> Love the LORD your God with all your heart and with all your soul and with all your strength.
>
> *Deuteronomy 6:4–5*

Life's purpose is to serve God and to prepare for the world to come.

C *The rainbow is a reminder of God's covenant with Noah after the flood*

Sikhism

Sikhism teaches that life is an opportunity to meditate on the wonder of a God who is always present, to discover that part of God which lies in each individual, and to gain enlightenment. The aim is to promote peace, equality and positive action in order that a person may grow towards achieving spiritual perfection, union with God and liberation from rebirth in the world.

AQA Examiner's tip

Make sure you are able to give examples of religious answers to questions about the meaning and purpose of life from the point of view of the religion(s) you have studied.

Discussion activity

With a partner, in a small group or as a class, discuss whether you think that there is a spiritual purpose and meaning to life. Make notes on the opinions given and the reasons for them.

Activities

1. Give examples of some the ultimate questions people ask about life.

2. Give three examples of life goals and beliefs about the purpose of life that people have. Say how important you think each one is.

3. 'No one knows the purpose and meaning of life.' What do you think? Explain your opinion.

Summary

You should now be able to explain what religious believers and others consider to be the meaning and purpose of life.

5.5 Image and views of 'self'

What does it mean to be you?

You may have been asked to give a description of yourself; for example, 'I am a son, an athlete, a friend …', and so on. It is often said that a person has three selves. There is the ideal self (what a person would like to be), the public self (the image a person thinks others have of them) and the real self (what a person is really like or really thinks about themselves). Sometimes, people would argue that what a person really thinks about himself or herself is not their real self. Others divide the self between what is the ego (the learned, superficial self of mind and body) and the true self (the spirit or soul of the person, such as the 'atman' in Hinduism).

What influences our self-image?

The opinions of family, friends and peers have an enormous influence on how we behave and how we think about ourselves. The images seen through television, advertisements and magazines have an effect on the way we see ourselves. Slogans like 'because you're worth it' encourage consumers to indulge themselves by buying the product that is being advertised. Some say that all this creates anxiety, promotes envy and encourages feelings of inadequacy and insecurity. Is this true, or do advertisements simply mirror society's values, encourage people to switch brands or inform people of new products and bargains?

What influences our views about self-worth?

People spend millions on make-up, designer clothes and keeping up with others. Models appear flawless, slim and without wrinkles or spots. Stars are used to endorse certain products, suggesting that to use them will so improve your **image** that you will become a winner rather than a loser. Those who do not meet these apparent expectations of physical attractiveness may have a low opinion of their **self-worth**, and this may result in negative behaviour, such as comfort eating. Others judge themselves by particular talents they have or do not possess, such as whether they are good at sport or academic studies. Most people respond to **peer pressure** and their self-esteem goes up or down depending on how well they fit into groups of people of their own age.

Religion and 'self'

Religions do not encourage a person to focus on 'self', or on his or her image, but to concentrate on spiritual things.

Buddhism

Buddhists believe that image and desire create craving, which results in dukkha (suffering).

> **Objectives**
> Consider questions concerning image, views of 'self' and self-worth.

> **Key terms**
> **Image**: a characteristic of a person or group concerning style, manner of dress and how one is, or wishes to be, perceived by others.
> **Self-worth**: valuing yourself as a person.
> **Peer pressure**: the influence of those from a similar age group who encourage a person to change their attitude or behaviour to conform to the group's beliefs or actions, regarding, for example, fashion sense.

Christianity

Christians believe that self has been corrupted by sin, so focusing on self appeals to sinful, human nature. Christianity teaches that Jesus rather than self needs to be at the centre of life. This is achieved by allowing Jesus' spirit to live within human beings, enabling people to concentrate on spiritual truth and serving others, rather than on self and image.

Hinduism

Hindus focus on the duties of the believer rather than the rights, image or self of the individual. This means that Hindus are under an obligation to consider the needs of others. The body will age and die but the karma resulting from either good or bad actions will result in either a good or bad reincarnation.

Islam

Muslims believe that the 'self' must submit to Allah's will and guidance, which is done by believing in his laws and acting upon them. This enables the believer to embrace qualities such as love, mercy, compassion, humility, forgiveness, sincerity, integrity and justice. Self, left unchecked, leads to wrong doing, which causes chaos, injustice and immorality and the triumph of evil. An example of reducing the importance of 'self' is practising modesty in dress.

Judaism

Jews believe that they are God's chosen people, made in God's image (Genesis 1:27). God made a covenant (agreement) with the Jews, agreeing to be their God but only if they worshipped no other god. The first four of the Ten Commandments set out this obligation (Exodus 20:3–7).

A *The Ten Commandments*

Sikhism

Sikhism teaches that birth in human form gives the opportunity to become morally perfect, to meditate on God's name, to earn final release from the cycle of rebirth and be reunited with God.

AQA Examiner's tip

Make sure you are able to describe the pressures on young people regarding image and explain religious attitudes to 'self' and image.

Discussion activity

With a partner, in a small group or as a class, discuss whether you think that it is possible not to be image conscious in today's world.

Activities

1. Explain what influences our self-image and feelings of self-worth.
2. Explain religious attitudes to image and 'self'.
3. 'Image gets in the way of faith because it's not seen as cool to be religious.' What do you think? Explain your opinion.

Summary

You should now understand religious and other attitudes to image, 'self' and self-worth.

5.6 Identity within faith communities (1)

Buddhism

Joining a sangha is the first step in identifying with Buddhism. Having attended services and retreats, and applied the teachings in everyday life, the formal part of becoming a Buddhist is undertaken during the affirmation or ordination ceremony.

The affirmation ceremony is unique to Shin Buddhism, which is a lay religious movement (not a religious order). A personal **commitment** is given to Pure Land Buddhism. A new Buddhist name is received and also an Affirmation Certificate.

A fully ordained monk conducts the Ordination Ceremony. Those wanting to join make a public announcement by repeating three times the Three Refuges. This states belief in the authority of the Buddha, the dhamma (teaching) and the sangha. The lay Buddhist can sometimes take Bodhisattva Vows. Males become known as upasaka (ordained follower) and females as upasika. The person receives a Buddhist name and becomes a formal member of the Buddhist community with a link to a monastic order. Later, lay Buddhists may wish to become monks (bhikkus) or nuns (bhikkhunis).

Buddhist monks live a simple and meditative lifestyle. Having entered the sangha, they follow the rules of conduct (approximately 227 rules for a male), as set out in the monastic codes (Vinaya). This means that they follow the example and teaching of the Buddha. The leader of the Tibetan Buddhists is the Dalai Lama, who makes statements on many moral issues, including the need for world peace. The chief monks give moral guidance to the monks in the monastery.

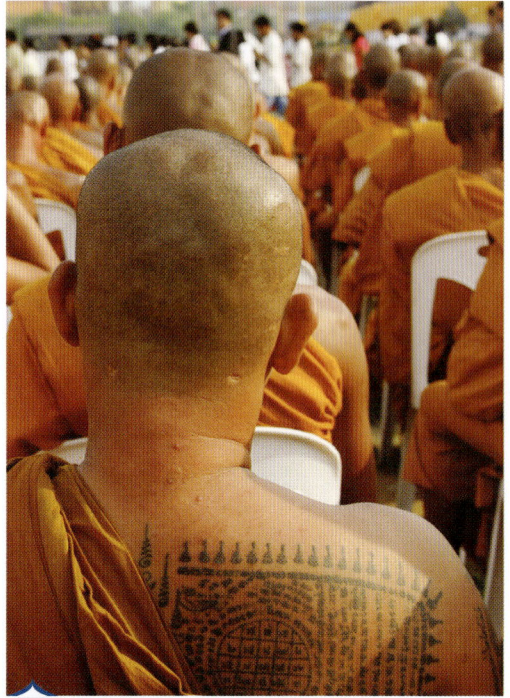

A Buddhist monks

> **Objectives**
> Investigate identity within faith communities, including ceremonies of commitment and the nature of leadership.

> **Key terms**
> **Commitment**: the state of being involved or obligated (in this case to a religious community).
> **Leadership**: religious leaders who guide and help followers in matters concerning their faith.

> **Research activity**
> 1. Use the internet or a library to find out about the Dalai Lama, leader of the Tibetan Buddhists, and his teaching on belonging to the Buddhist community.

> **Extension activity**
> Using the internet or a library, find out more about infant and believers' baptism, confirmation, and the role of the Pope in the Roman Catholic Church.

> **Research activity**
> 2. Use the internet or a library to find more information about becoming a Hindu monk, or about the samskaras.

Christianity

Christianity has many denominations (churches) with different beliefs, customs and traditions. Most denominations have a ceremony of infant baptism, when a child is accepted to join the Christian community. Parents and godparents make promises on the child's behalf, which are renewed by the individual at confirmation or when they become members of the church. Christians teach that all believers are brothers and sisters in Christ.

Some denominations, such as Baptists, prefer believer's baptism. The believer explains why they wish to be a Christian and then is momentarily submerged under water as a sign of washing away their old, sinful nature.

For Roman Catholics (the largest Christian denomination), the Bishop of Rome (the Pope) is believed to be Jesus' representative on earth. On his death, the cardinals elect a new pope. In the Anglican Church, the Archbishop of Canterbury is the most important bishop. The British king or queen is the official Head of the Church of England, but the real power is with the Archbishop and bishops. Christianity has a **leadership** including priests, rectors, vicars, ministers and pastors (the titles vary according to the denomination). It also has voluntary lay leaders.

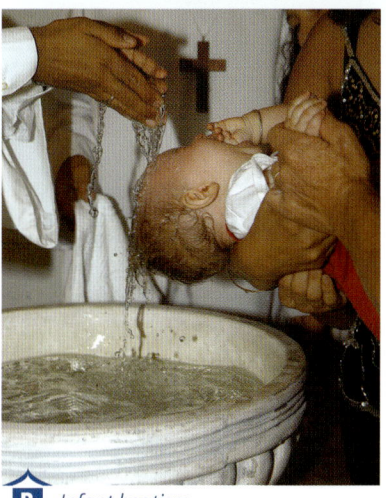

B *Infant baptism*

Hinduism

In the Hindu community, 16 major samskaras (rites) are performed by the brahmins (priests). These include the birth (jatakarma) and naming (namakarana) ceremonies and the sacred thread ceremony (upanayanam). The age at which the sacred thread ceremony occurs depends on the caste of the individual and only boys who come from the top three castes undergo the ceremony. During the ceremony, the secret of life is taught by revealing the nature of Brahman, the Ultimate Reality. The individual wears the sacred thread, which is tied end to end with one knot, on the left shoulder, and wrapped around the body underneath the right arm. The day of the ceremony is chosen by an astrologer (someone who looks for meaning in the stars). The thread is white, red or yellow and is a sign of adulthood and religious maturity. The strands symbolise the duties associated with belonging to the Hindu community, that is: to worship god, to love and respect one's parents, and to listen to one's religious teacher.

The Hindu religious leaders are from the Brahmin varna and the six duties of a brahmin are: teaching; study; performing worship and ritual of sacrifice to the gods; making the sacrificial fire into which offerings are poured; and accepting and giving alms (donations of food or money to the poor).

AQA Examiner's tip

You do not have to study more than one religion but if you do know about more than one it may help you to understand the basic principles of what it means to belong to a community based on a religious faith.

Discussion activity

With a partner, in a small group or as a class, discuss the value of ceremonies of commitment, such as the sacred thread ceremony in Hinduism, or confirmation in Christianity. Make notes on the opinions given.

Summary

You should now be able to describe how a person becomes identified with a religious community, and the role of religious leaders within that community.

Activities

1. Describe the roles of leaders in the religion(s) you are studying.

2. 'You should not join a religious community until you are at least 16.' What do you think? Explain your opinion.

5.7 Identity within faith communities (2)

Judaism

Traditionally, anyone who has a Jewish mother or who follows the Jewish faith or has converted to Judaism in accordance with Jewish Law has a Jewish identity. On the eighth day of a baby boy's life, a religious ceremony of circumcision, called Brit Milah, takes place to welcome the child into the covenant between God and the Jews.

Around the age of puberty, a coming of age ceremony is held which signifies that the person is mature enough to take responsibility for his or her actions. Before the Bar Mitzvah (for boys) and Bat Mitzvah (for girls), the parents, following the Jewish law and **traditions**, are responsible for the child. Generally, this is celebrated at the age of 13 for boys and 12 for girls, although in many Conservative and Reform synagogues girls celebrate their Bat Mitzvahs at the age of 13. In non-Orthodox synagogues the young man or woman reads a portion of the Torah. A celebration meal follows the ceremony.

In Orthodox Judaism only men are rabbis but, since the 20th century, Reform Jews have accepted women as rabbis. Rabbis are highly trained in Jewish law, are experts on the Torah and act as teachers on central matters within Judaism.

Islam

When a child is born to Muslim parents, the call to prayer (adhan) is recited in his or her right ear and the call to stand up for prayer (iqamah) is recited in the left ear. The parents believe that it is their duty to teach their child the beliefs of Islam and, at the age of four or five, the Bismillah ceremony takes place. The child recites the first five verses of the Qur'an and writes the Arabic alphabet. The education into the traditions and customs of Islam continue, including preparing for and learning the five daily prayers (salat). Being part of the **brotherhood** or sisterhood is an important part of Islam. The community of believers is known as the Ummah.

Questions are answered and guidance given to the local Muslim community by the imam, who is the leader of the mosque. He (women are not allowed to become imams) also leads the prayers and preaches to the community. In some countries, such as Iran, the title 'ayatollah' is given to those who are experts in Islamic studies and who usually teach in religious colleges.

Sikhism

Soon after birth, if a child is to be baptised, the Guru Granth Sahib is opened and the first letter of the first word on the left-hand page determines the first letter of the child's name. Amrit (water and sugar) is placed on the child's lips and prayers are said from the japji and ardas. The sharing of karah parshad signifies entry into the Sikh community.

Objectives
Investigate identity within faith communities, including ceremonies of commitment and the nature of leadership.

A A young man at his Bar Mitzvah

Research activity

1. Use the internet or a library find out more about how Bar and Bat Mitzvah is celebrated, and its significance. Record your findings.

Extension activity
Use the internet or a library to find out more about the importance of the Ummah.

At some point in life, non-baptised Sikhs may wish to be baptised and become Khalsa Sikhs. This requires them to speak, read and recite from the Guru Granth Sahib and to promise to follow a strict code of conduct, including not cutting their hair. They wear the 5Ks as a symbol of their faith, one of which is a turban to control their uncut hair.

B *The turban is one of the 5Ks*

Equality is important in Sikhism and there is no special ceremony to initiate a baptised Sikh as a granthi (leader). The granthi looks after the Guru Granth Sahib in the gurdwara and performs the ceremonial opening of the holy book in the morning and the closing of it in the evening. The granthi leads the morning and evening services.

C *Inside a gurdwara, showing the throne for the Guru Granth Sahib*

Key terms

Traditions: the handing down of customs from one generation to another.

Brotherhood: group that offers companionship, help, and support to each other.

Research activity

2 Using the internet or a library, find out more about the Khalsa.

AQA Examiner's tip

Make sure you are able to use some religious technical terms in the correct context (place) for the religion(s) you are studying.

Discussion activity

With a partner, in a small group or as a whole class, discuss the qualities you think a religious leader should possess. Make notes on the opinions given and the reasons for them.

Activities

1 Describe an initiation ceremony within a religion you are studying.

2 'Joining a religious community gives a person a real sense of belonging and identity.' What do you think? Explain your opinion.

Summary

You should now be able to describe how a person becomes identified with a religious community, and explain the role of religious leaders within that community.

5.8 Symbolism and dress

■ Religious identification

The religion of believers may be identified by the clothing or **symbols** they wear.

Buddhism

Buddhist monks and nuns are recognised by their robes. These are made of one piece of cloth and their function is simply to protect the body. As dark red was the cheapest colour in Kashmir, Tibetan monks wear red robes. In most parts of South East Asia the robes are an orange colour (saffron) worn over a red undergarment, but in Japan the robe is traditionally black, grey or blue. Buddhist priests in China and Japan wear a skullcap.

Christianity

The clergy (priests) in many Christian denominations wear clerical clothes even when not taking a service. For men, this usually consists of a suit with black shirt with a white, reversed collar. At services vestments are worn. These include a cassock, surplice, preaching scarf and a stole (a narrow garment draped around the neck and hanging down in front of the wearer). Monks and nuns wear a habit, which usually has a hood for men, and a long dress with a fitted head covering for nuns. Christians may wear the symbol of a cross or fish.

Hinduism

Traditional clothing for a baby is a cap and a balut (triangular piece of cloth). For adults, the dress code has historically depended on caste. The most common dress for a workman was a loincloth, with a woman wearing a sari. Many Hindus wear a tilaka as an acknowledgement that they are the Lord Krisha's servant; these clay marks may be worn on different parts of the body. The bindi is a dot worn by women on the forehead. Hindu brides use henna, a dark red/brown vegetable dye, to make intricate designs on the palms of their hands to bring good fortune.

> **Objectives**
> Investigate how the identity of a religious believer may be reflected through symbols and what they wear.

> **Key terms**
> **Symbol**: an object, image or action that represents something else.
> **Custom**: accepted or habitual practice, usually of long standing.

> **Research activity**
> Choose one of the following, and use the internet or a library to discover the significance of the symbols or clothing that they wear: Buddhist monks, Christian clergy, Muslim women, Hindu castes, Hasidic Jews or Khalsa Sikhs.

A Hindu woman with bindi

Islam

The Qur'an insists that Muslims dress modestly. Men must cover themselves between the navel and the knees, and some wear a topi (skullcap). A woman's clothing should hang loose so that the shape of the body is not apparent, with only her hands and face showing. A variety of headdresses are worn (hejab or hijab). Some Muslim women also wear a veil.

> **Beliefs and teachings**
>
> And say to the believing women that they should lower their gaze and guard their modesty that they should not display their beauty.
>
> *Qur'an 24:31*

Judaism

As a sign of respect for God, Jewish men (and some women in Conservative and Reform communities) wear a skullcap called a kippah. Women may wear a scarf covering the head. For morning worship in the synagogue, the men wear a silk or wool prayer robe called a tallit. It is similar to a shawl with tassels, which represent Jewish Laws. To remind them to love God, many wear a tefillin or phylacteries. These are two small leather boxes containing scriptures, one worn on the forehead and the other on the arm. Customs vary between the different branches of Judaism. For example, some pious (Hasidic) Jews wear long sidelocks because they interpret the law to mean that the temple should not be shaved at all. Others wear a beard and sideburns because they want to follow the law exactly.

B *Orthodox Jews at the Western Wailing Wall in Jerusalem*

Sikhism

Khalsa Sikhs, male and female, wear the 5Ks to symbolise their membership of the Sikh faith. Kesh is the term for the uncut hair, but turbans are worn to keep the long hair covered and tidy. It is a mark of dedication showing acceptance of God's will. Under the turban, two combs (kanghas) are used to hold the hair in place. The third K is the kara, a steel bracelet which reflects the idea that God has no beginning or end. A small sword (kirpan) is worn and kachera, which are undergarments.

AQA Examiner's tip

Make sure that you know the technical terms for the articles of clothing worn in at least one religion.

Discussion activity

With a partner, in a small group or as a class, discuss what you think about believers wearing symbols of their faith. Make notes on the opinions given.

Activities

1. How might believers recognise members of their faith?

2. Give two examples of religious clothing and explain their significance.

3. 'It must be hard to wear a religious uniform.' What do you think? Explain your opinion.

Summary

You should now be able to explain how some believers identify with their faith through the symbols or clothes they wear.

5.9 Healthy living and sacred writings

■ Healthy living

To a religious believer, being healthy is a state of complete physical, mental, social and spiritual wellbeing. This means the whole person working as one to achieve good health and happiness. Religions encourage **healthy living**; for example, eating the right foods and getting physically fit. Some of the religious food laws were designed to prevent illness. Smoking is not encouraged and alcohol, if allowed, is permitted only in moderation.

The health of the mind (mental health) and our emotions are also important. Without positive thoughts, viewpoints and the cultivation of a positive self-image, people may see themselves as being of little value and become depressed. Being able to handle normal levels of stress, deal with difficult situations, recover from setbacks, and feel capable and competent are all signs of good mental health.

Religions believe in the sanctity of life and teach that it is important to give and receive love, compassion and forgiveness, to experience laughter and joy, and to develop positive relationships. Teachings, such as 'So God created man in his own image' (Genesis 1:27), illustrate the value religions put on human life. Healthy living is, therefore, necessary to fulfil God's purpose in life.

■ Sacred writings

Sacred writings give advice about spiritual matters and the way to live. Laws and teachings guide believers to act in a way that creates positive karma or develops a close relationship with God. Religious believers look to the sacred texts for guidance on moral or ethical issues. For example, if they are faced with a decision such as 'Is it right or wrong to get drunk?', or 'Is it right to have sex outside marriage?', they will find relevant teachings in the scriptures.

Buddhism

Buddhists have the Tripitaka (The Three Baskets) that consists of the Vinaya Pitaka (discipline), Sutta Pitaka (themes) and Abhidhamma Pitaka (analysis). The Vinaya Pitaka is the oldest part and gives Buddha's teaching on issues like living in peace, caring for the old and giving to charity. The Sutta Pitaka contains the Dhammapada verses, which were spoken by the Buddha on moral issues. The Abhidhamma Pitaka explains the teachings of the Sutta Pitaka.

Christianity

Christians refer to the Old or New Testaments of the Bible, which consists of 66 books. The first four books of the New Testament (gospels) include the teachings of Jesus, such as the Sermon on the Mount (Matthew 5–7). Many of St Paul's letters to the early Church include guidance on moral issues. Christians regard the Bible as the inspired and active word of God (Hebrews 4:12).

> **Objectives**
> Investigate beliefs about healthy living.
>
> Investigate the sacred writings and their guidance on how to live.

> **Key terms**
> **Healthy living**: living a life which is good for the body, both physically and mentally.

> **Research activity**
> Use the internet or a library to find out more about the sacred writings for the religion(s) you are studying. Make notes on some of the guidance they contain on how to live.

> **links**
> The term 'sanctity of life' is defined in the Glossary at the back of this book.

> **AQA Examiner's tip**
> Make sure you have at least a basic knowledge of the sacred texts and their guidance on how to live for the religion(s) you are studying.

Chapter 5   Religion and identity   113

Hinduism

Hindus have the shruti (revealed) scriptures, which include the Rig Veda, Sama Veda, Yajur Veda and Atharva Veda. The smriti (remembered) scriptures include the Puranas, the Mahabharata (includes the Bhagavad Gita) and Ramayana (epics), the Laws of Manu, Tantras and Darshana literature.

Judaism

Jews consult the Tenakh (the scriptures Christians refer to as the Old Testament) and in particular the Torah (the Law). This includes the Ten Commandments, which are also important to Christians. In addition, they have the Talmud (teachings), which is made up of the Mishnah (the oral law as it was written down) and the Gemara (commentaries on the laws).

A Torah scrolls

Islam

Muslims believe that the Qur'an is Allah's word and so is an infallible source of authority. Also the Hadith, which includes sayings of Muhammad, is used as it contains rules of life and teachings about ethical issues.

Sikhism

Sikhs use the Guru Granth Sahib (also known as the Adi Granth), containing the writings of the earlier gurus. It is regarded as the source of knowledge, truth and wisdom and is treated as a living guru.

Summary

You should now be able to explain religious attitudes to healthy living, and give examples of sacred writings and their guidance on how to live.

Discussion activity

With a partner, in a small group or as a class discuss whether you agree with the following statement: 'Healthy living has nothing to do with religion.' Make notes on the opinions given and the reasons for them.

Activities

1. Explain how and why religions support the idea of healthy living.

2. 'Sacred writings were written too long ago to be of much practical help in deciding how to live today.' What do you think? Explain your opinion.

B Muslim girl holding a Qur'an

5.10 Interdependence and decision making

Decision making

It is not always easy to make wise or right decisions, and on occasions help and guidance is needed. Advice might be sought from family members, such as parents. All major religions recognise the wisdom associated with experience and age; for example, 'Honour your father and mother' (Exodus 20:12). Friends and peers (people of the same age) are another source of advice, and religious believers also turn to their faith community.

An important part of a religious leader's role is that of counselling. Buddhist monks, Christian clergy, Hindu priests, Muslim imams, Jewish rabbis and Sikh granthis are a prominent source of religious authority that is accessible to believers of all ages in their faith communities. They give advice, taking into account the sacred writings, traditions and practices of the faith. Some modern problems are not specifically mentioned in the sacred writings, but religious leaders will draw on the principles that have been laid down. They also use their own experience when attempting to give guidance.

> **Objectives**
>
> Understand sources which are used to help in decision making.
>
> Understand concepts of interdependence and multiple identities.

A Christian minister

B Jewish Rabbi

Ultimately, the individual has to make the decision. Religious believers may pray and listen to their **conscience**. A decision to do something against his or her moral values can leave a person feeling uncomfortable. On the other hand, they may experience a feeling of integrity or 'wholeness' when their actions conform to their beliefs. The sense of right or wrong is often referred to as the voice of conscience and many believers say that it is God-given.

Interdependence and multiple identities

The phrase 'It's a small world!' is often used to emphasise the idea that we are living in an international society or global village. A century ago, it took months to travel to the other side of the world; now it takes less than a day. By email or telephone, worldwide communication is virtually instant. Actions taken by people in this country affect individuals thousands of miles away. 'Think globally, act locally' is a slogan used to illustrate our **interdependence** and the need for everyone to do their part with regard to sustainable development and reducing global warming. Many believe in an interconnection which sees a 'oneness' in all things.

Each person has **multiple identities**. We have our own unique names but we are also members of a family, and are either male or female. We are also members of our community (for example, village, town or city), and many people belong to a club or society. Each individual is from a particular ethnic group, may belong to a particular religion, lives in a region and a country, which is part of a continent, and we are all citizens of planet Earth.

Key terms

Conscience: the inner feeling of right or wrong that governs a person's actions.

Interdependence: when two or more things depend on each other.

Multiple identities: several identities; for example, daughter, sports captain, Northerner, Briton.

Discussion activity

With a partner, in a small group or as a class, list and discuss your multiple identities.

Research activity

Research sources, e.g. sacred texts, family, leaders, used in decision making by the religious believers in the religion(s) you are studying and provide examples of decisions which might be based on their guidance.

Extension activity

Use the internet to find out more about the slogan 'Think globally, act locally'. What does it mean? Record examples of how people are putting this idea into practice.

Activities

1. List the sources of guidance which are available to religious believers and explain their importance.
2. Explain what is meant by 'interdependence' and 'multiple identities'.
3. 'What I do doesn't matter, as the world is such a big place.' What do you think? Explain your opinion.

Summary

You should now be able to identify sources which are used to help in decision making, and explain why each person has several identities.

AQA Examiner's tip

Make sure that you understand the meaning of 'conscience' and its application to religious believers.

Assessment guidance

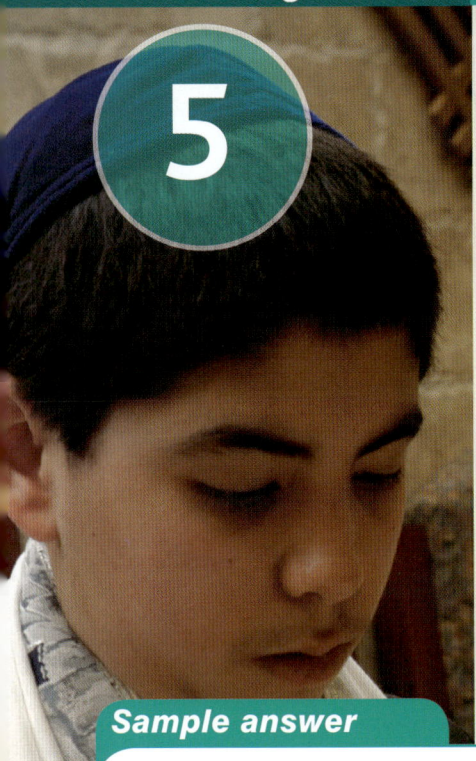

5

Religion and identity – summary

For the examination you should now be able to:

- ✔ explain what it means to be human
- ✔ explain physical and spiritual dimensions of life and personhood
- ✔ evaluate religious ideas about the purpose and meaning of life
- ✔ discuss issues concerning image, 'self' and self-worth
- ✔ describe how identity is celebrated in a faith community
- ✔ explain how a believer may be identified through symbolism and dress
- ✔ explain religious attitudes to healthy living
- ✔ understand and evaluate religious sources used in decision making
- ✔ explain the concepts of interdependence and multiple identities.

Sample answer

1. Write an answer to the following exam question:

   'The physical part of life is far more important than the spiritual part.'

   Do you agree? Give reasons for your answer, showing that you have thought about more than one point of view.

   (6 marks)

2. Read the following sample answer.

   Atheists would agree with this statement because they do not believe in a spiritual dimension. Looking after the body and its needs is seen as far more important than something that doesn't exist. We can see the benefits of looking after our health and enjoying life now.

   Theists would argue that the spiritual part of life is not only important now but also involves our afterlife. Muslims say that this life is just a test and preparation for the next, so the spiritual part of life is something we all should be very concerned about. Christians might quote Mark who says, 'What good is it for a man to gain the whole world, yet forfeit his soul?' (Mark 8:36). Personally I think that we should be concerned about both the physical and spiritual.

3. With a partner, discuss the sample answer. Do you think that there are other things that the student could have included in the answer?

4. What mark (out of 6) would you give this answer? (Look at the mark scheme in the Introduction on page 7 (AO2) before you attempt this.) What are the reasons for the mark you have given?

AQA Examination-style questions

1   Look at the photograph and answer the following questions.

   (a) What is meant by 'self-worth'? *(2 marks)*

   (b) Describe two ways a believer may show his or her religious identity. *(4 marks)*

   (c) 'Religious believers should not be concerned about their image.' What do you think? Explain your opinion. *(3 marks)*

   (d) Give three different sources which may help a religious believer in making a decision. *(3 marks)*

   (e) 'We will never know the meaning and purpose of life.' Do you agree? Give reasons for your answer, showing that you have thought about more than one point of view. Refer to religious arguments in your answer. *(6 marks)*

> **AQA Examiner's tip**
> Remember when you are asked if you agree with a statement you must show what you think and the reasons why other people might take a different view. If your answer is one sided, you will achieve a maximum of 4 marks. If you make no comment about religious belief or practice, you will achieve no more than 3 marks.

6 Religion and human rights

6.1 Rights and responsibilities

Objectives
Consider a person's rights and responsibilities.

Rights abuses

A Bullying is an abuse of human rights

In some communities, some people are looked down upon and even picked on, and no one does anything about it. This bullying might happen because of race, colour, religion, age, sex or because the victims have a disability. It is not their fault, but they are treated as second-class citizens. They live in an unfair world and are unable to enjoy the same freedoms as everyone else. In extreme cases this unfair treatment can lead to terrible persecution and even death through ethnic cleansing (when one racial group tries to eliminate a different racial group). This happened in the Second World War when the Nazis murdered around six million Jews in the gas chambers. Persecution of minority religious groups has often led to torture and martyrdom. Some groups have been treated as subhuman, such as Africans who in the 18th and early 19th centuries were sold like cattle into slavery.

Development of rights

Some citizens do not have a voice to fight for them, so other people have tried to do so on their behalf. Over the centuries there has gradually come a realisation that everyone should have **rights** and should be protected from abuse. The first real attempt to protect human rights came in Britain with the signing of the Magna Carta by King John in 1215. This gave people rights including, for example, the right not to be imprisoned without a fair trial (the right of Habeas Corpus).

Key terms

Rights: entitlements that all people should have.

Responsibility: the legal or moral duty which a person has.

links

You can find out more about the Human Rights Act on page 123.

Gradually, Parliament introduced laws to protect people. For example, the Bill of Rights (1689) granted:

- freedom to petition the monarch
- freedom to elect members of parliament without the interference of the monarch
- freedom of speech in Parliament
- freedom from a monarch's interference in the law
- freedom from the monarch setting taxes (Parliament had to agree to any new taxes)
- freedom from cruel punishment
- freedom from fines or property being confiscated without trial.

B *Members of Parliament pass laws to protect human rights*

In 1807 Parliament passed an act to abolish the Slave Trade, and in 1833 the Slavery Abolition Act gave all slaves in the British Empire their freedom. Also in the 19th century, various acts of Parliament limited the working hours of children in factories and mines. For example, the Cotton Mills and Factories Act 1819 stated that no children under the age of nine were to be employed and anyone between the ages of 9–16 could not work more than 12 hours per day. The Factory Act of 1878 stated that no child under 10 could be employed and that 10–14 year olds should not work for more than half days. Christian MPs were very involved in getting the law changed. Other acts of Parliament have given children the right to an education, and the Human Rights Act became law in 2000.

Responsibilities

With rights also go **responsibilities**. If it is right for a person to have freedom of speech, then with this right goes a moral responsibility not to cause hatred or provoke violence by what the person says. Or, in a class situation at school, where a subject is being debated, there is the responsibility not to stop others from expressing their ideas and being listened to. The responsibilities of being a citizen include respecting the rights of everyone else and obeying the law. In 1991 the United Nations set out the rights of children in the Convention on the Rights of the Child. In it children are asked to respect each other in a humane way. If children have the right to be protected from cruelty, exploitation and neglect, they also have a responsibility not to bully or harm each other. If children expect to live in a clean environment, they should help to look after it. The same principle applies to each of the rights, including the duty to respect other people's religious beliefs.

AQA Examiner's tip

Appreciate that there is a link between being given rights and having responsibilities.

Discussion activity

With a partner, in a small group or as a whole class, discuss and make a list of the responsibilities that each citizen has.

Activities

1. Explain some of the reasons why it is necessary to have human rights.

2. Give three examples of the laws that have been made to protect human rights in Britain.

3. 'The most important right is only to be punished after a fair trial.' What do you think? Explain your opinion.

Summary

You should now be able to explain why laws have been passed that have given people rights, and the importance of citizens acting responsibly towards others.

6.2 Religious attitudes towards the law and human rights

In addition to state law, religions also have their own laws and rules, which have an impact on the rights and responsibilities of citizens who belong to the faith groups.

Buddhism

The Buddha said that monks should obey the law of the land, but this advice has been difficult in countries like Tibet, where human rights violations have taken place since the Chinese invasion. Following the Noble Eightfold Path, which includes Right Action, is important to Buddhists. Buddhists believe in justice; for example, if someone has broken the law, the situation is not resolved until all those concerned are happy with the court's decision and those who have suffered are compensated. The Law of Karma (every action must have a reaction, an effect) discourages a person from actions that will result in suffering, and this encourages Buddhists to support the law and human rights.

Christianity

St Paul wrote:

> **Beliefs and teachings**
>
> Let everyone be subject to the governing authorities, for there is no authority except that which God has established. The authorities that exist have been established by God.
>
> *Romans 13:1*

This means that the law should be obeyed because it is right, not simply because it is the law. Sometimes the law needs to be changed in the interest of human rights and justice. The crucifixion of Jesus was legal, but it was not just. Christians believe that human beings have rights because God loves people and 'created man in his own image' (Genesis 1:27). Respect for all human beings means that all are treated fairly.

Islam

Muslim law is based upon four sources: the Qur'an, the Sunnah (practices of the Prophet Muhammad), the agreed view of Islamic scholars and new case law, which has been decided by Shari'ah judges. All laws must in essence agree with the teachings in the Qur'an, and only if the Qur'an does not deal directly with a subject do Muslims look at alternative sources of Islamic law. Shari'ah Law includes protecting some human rights; for example, the life and property of all citizens in an Islamic country are considered sacred, and insulting or making fun of others is forbidden.

Objectives

Find out about religious attitudes towards the law and human rights.

Key terms

- **Law (The)**: a system of rules enforced by a country's legal system with consequences for those who break them.
- **Human rights**: the basic rights and freedoms to which all human beings should be entitled.

A *In addition to state law, religions also have their own laws and rules*

Hinduism

Traditional Hinduism, which considers Manu's Dharma Sutra as the authority, relates all human rights to a person's caste, age and sex. Rights are then privileges of status and position; for example, Brahmans have many more rights than untouchables. Many modern Hindus see human rights quite differently. Gandhi, for example, believed that every Hindu should fulfil their duty (dharma), which meant that all the community had rights and responsibilities. Gandhi believed in human dignity and that all people have an equal right to the necessities of life. Where the law did not allow this, Gandhi advocated passive resistance as a means of obtaining justice.

AQA Examiner's tip

Be clear about the attitudes of the religion(s) you are studying to the law and to human rights.

Judaism

The Torah (first five books of the Tenakh) sets out God's law. Six hundred and thirteen commands were given to the Israelites, including the Ten Commandments (see Exodus 20). Obedience to the law of God is seen as a duty and extremely important as it is part of the covenant with him. Sin and breaking the law breaks the relationship with God.

Beliefs and teachings

I desire to do your will, my God; your law is within my heart.

Psalms 40:8

Jews believe it important to obey the laws of the land (unless it takes away their right to religious freedom). Jewish attitudes to human rights are based on the belief that every life is precious and sacred to God.

Discussion activity

With a partner, in a small group or as a whole class, discuss whether you think state laws or religious laws are the most important. Make notes on the opinions given and the reasons for them.

B *Reading the Torah scrolls*

Activities

1. What is the difference between a country's legal system and religious laws?

2. Explain why religions agree with the idea that humans should have rights.

3. 'Follow religious laws and everyone's human rights would be protected.' What do you think? Explain your opinion.

Sikhism

Sikhs have struggled to obtain equal human rights. Many have been persecuted or have lived in societies where the state laws have not supported Sikh rules. For example, Sikhs in France were banned from wearing turbans when being photographed for ID documents and they appealed to the European Court of Human Rights in Strasbourg. Sikhs believe that truthfulness is the core of daily life and that the noblest conduct is to practise selfless love, compassion and mercy.

They believe that by following the teaching, 'I am a friend to all; I am everyone's friend' (Guru Granth Sahib 671), everyone's human rights will be protected.

Summary

You should now be able to explain the attitudes of the religion(s) you have studied to the law and to human rights.

6.3 Human rights legislation

The Universal Declaration of Human Rights (UDHR)

The **Universal Declaration of Human Rights** (UDHR) was adopted by the United Nations General Assembly in 1948. It consists of 30 articles or rights, on which later discussion of human rights has been based. The aim was to agree minimum rights for every human being in every country of the world, so that everyone could enjoy freedom, justice and peace. It recognises the dignity and worth of each individual, promotes equality for men and women and prohibits persecution. All the member countries of the United Nations (UN) signed the declaration, but there are still several countries that do not follow the rules and the UN has few powers to force them to do so.

Religious believers were very much involved in the development of the Declaration. Pope Paul VI expressed his desire for a common ideal, which would help to make the world more peaceful after the Second World War. In 1943, Protestant Christians in the USA began working to establish religious freedom, and the following year involved leaders of churches in other countries. Jews also became involved in drafting a declaration of human rights. The UN built on the work that had been done by setting up a Commission on Human Rights, chaired by Eleanor Roosevelt, which declared that the UDHR was a moral and spiritual milestone for the world.

Objectives

Find out about the Universal Declaration of Human Rights and the Human Rights Act.

Key terms

United Nations Declaration of Human Rights: document produced by the United Nations setting out the rights that all people should be entitled to.

Human Rights Act: an act of parliament passed in 1998 which says that all organisations have a duty to protect the rights of all individuals in the UK.

The Universal Declaration of Human Rights, 1948

Article 1	All human beings are born free and equal in dignity and rights. They are endowed with reason and conscience and should act towards one another in a spirit of brotherhood.
Article 2	Everyone is entitled to all the rights and freedoms set forth in this Declaration, without distinction of any kind, such as race, colour, sex, language, religion, political or other opinion, national or social origin, property, birth or other status ….
Article 11 (1)	Everyone charged with a penal offence has the right to be presumed innocent until proved guilty according to law in a public trial at which he has had all the guarantees necessary for his defence.
Article 18	Everyone has the right to freedom of thought, conscience and religion ….

A *United Nations Headquarters, New York City, USA*

Extension activity

Use the internet or a library to find out more about the UDHR and the thirty articles. Choose three of interest and record them.

Chapter 6 Religion and human rights

B *Article 26: Everyone has the right to education*

AQA Examiner's tip
Know some specific examples of rights given by the UDHR and HRA and be able to explain their importance.

Discussion activity
With a partner, in a small group or as a whole class, discuss how important you feel it is for every country to allow their citizens to have all the rights that are included in the Universal Declaration of Human Rights. Consider issues like justice, persecution, dignity and the value of the individual. Make notes on the opinions given and the reasons for them.

The Human Rights Act (HRA)

The **Human Rights Act** was passed by the UK Parliament in 1998 and came into force in October 2000. The aim was to add to UK law the rights contained in the European Convention on Human Rights, so that UK courts could deal with the breach of a right without the need to go to the European Court of Human Rights in Strasbourg. The basic rights set out in the HRA include the right to life, liberty, security, privacy, marriage, family life, free elections, education, fair trial and the right not to be held guilty of a criminal offence which did not exist in law at the time at which it was committed. It prohibits the use of torture, slavery and forced labour and gives the freedom for people to meet together, express views, act according to conscience and have a free choice of religion. The HRA affects public authorities, courts and tribunals, future laws and individuals. The majority of the rights contained in the Act are limited or qualified, which means that in certain circumstances, one person's right may not be defended if another's right is taken away. For example, a person's right to freedom of speech would not be supported if they expressed views that stirred up racial hatred, harming other people.

Activities

1. Explain three of the articles included in the Universal Declaration of Human Rights.

2. Give some examples of the rights given in the Human Rights Act.

3. 'People focus too much on their human rights and not enough on religious duty.' What do you think? Explain your opinion.

Summary
You should now know and be able to explain some of the rights outlined in the Universal Declaration of Human Rights and the Human Rights Act.

6.4 Children's rights and support

Children's rights

In 1989, the United Nations decided that young people under the age of 18 need special care and protection from people who ignore their human rights. The Convention on the Rights of the Child consists of 54 articles spelling out basic rights that children everywhere should have. These were designed to: help young people have the best opportunities to develop their potential; help young people to be able to participate in family, cultural and social life; and to protect them from harmful influences, including sexual **abuse** and exploitation. Standards were set in health care, education, legal, civil and social services. The Convention includes the following articles:

Objectives

Investigate children's rights.

Find out about support for victims of human rights abuses.

Key terms

Abuse: the harmful treatment of someone; the bad or wrong use of something.

Legal rights: rights that are laid down as an entitlement by law.

The Convention on the Rights of the Child, 1989

Article 12 Children have the right to say what they think should happen, when adults are making decisions that affect them, and to have their opinions taken in account.

Article 19 Governments should ensure that children are properly cared for, and protect them from violence, abuse and neglect by their parents, or anyone else who looks after them.

Article 31 All children have a right to relax and play, and to join in a wide range of activities.

A *No child should have to suffer abuse*

Nearly all countries have adopted these articles and agreed laws that give children **legal rights**. The United Nations Children's Fund (UNICEF), which works to uphold the Convention on the Rights of the Child and to protect children's rights in 155 countries worldwide, monitors this.

Examiner's tip
Be prepared to explain why it is important that there are organisations to help victims of abuse.

Extension activity
Using the internet or a library, find out more about children's rights and record three examples of rights which you find interesting or which you did not know before.

Support for children

Some young people have many problems and difficulties in their lives. Sometimes, the issues are serious abuses of human rights, such as physical violence, but often there are other worries such as relationship problems at school, feelings of isolation or concerns about the future. There is no need to suffer in silence, as help is available. Discussing problems with a trained counsellor can be a great help and many people get pastoral support from the faith communities to which they belong. However, it is not always easy to speak face to face with someone, and some people prefer to talk about sensitive issues to a person who has been trained to listen and to help via the telephone (see the ChildLine case study).

Research activity
1. Use the internet to research what the ChildLine slogan is. Consider why it uses this slogan.
2. For the religion(s) you are studying find out what it teaches about the importance of children and their rights.

ChildLine
In the 1980s, TV presenter Esther Rantzen suggested to the BBC that a child watch organisation needed to be set up to help young people with problems. This resulted in the emergence of ChildLine, a charity associated with the National Society for the Prevention of Cruelty to Children (NSPCC), providing a free 24-hour counselling service for young people. All calls to the help line are kept confidential, and several thousands of phone calls are received daily. Thousands of volunteers have been trained to answer the calls and deal sympathetically with issues like physical and sexual abuse, pregnancy, HIV and AIDS, bullying, worries about school or the future, concerns about parents or family members, friends, isolation and running away from home. If the counsellors are unable to help personally, they will supply contact details of someone who will be able to assist.

B *ChildLine can be contacted on 0800 1111*

Activities
1. Explain what is meant by the abuse of children's rights.
2. Give two examples of children's rights found in the Convention on the Rights of the Child.
3. 'Being able to speak confidentially is the greatest benefit of ChildLine.' What do you think? Explain your opinion.

Summary
You should now be able to explain the work of ChildLine and how young people are able to obtain help if they have a problem, or if their human rights are being ignored or violated.

6.5 Citizen's Advice and the Samaritans

Sometimes, individuals do not know what to do to protect their human rights. For example, he or she may have purchased some faulty goods, but the company who sold it to them may not be willing to refund their money or replace the product. In circumstances like this, a person may need advice and may not be able to afford a solicitor. The Citizens Advice Bureau was set up to provide free advice.

Citizens Advice

The Citizens Advice service (also known as CAB because it used to be called the Citizens' Advice Bureau) began in the Second World War. It has now developed into one of the UK's biggest voluntary organisations with branches in over 3,000 locations. Over 20,000 volunteer workers and several thousand paid staff provide services for all sections of the community. In most branches there is a paid manager, advice session supervisors, advisers and sometimes specialist paid advisers. The organisation is funded mainly from membership fees, grants from local authorities and central government.

Objectives
Investigate the work of the Citizens Advice and the Samaritans.

links
The terms 'justice' and 'empowerment' are defined in the Glossary at the back of this book.

Extension activity
1. Use the internet to find out about Crossline, which is a Christian counselling service. Make notes on the work Crossline does.

A *The Citizens Advice service (formally the Citizens Advice Bureau) helps people resolve their legal, money and other problems*

The Citizens Advice service has two main aims:
- To help individuals know their rights and responsibilities, to be aware of the services available to them and to ensure that their needs are expressed effectively. In other words, to be able to obtain justice for the individual whatever the situation may be.
- To influence the development of local and national social policies and services to benefit all citizens.

The service includes advice given face to face within the community, by telephone, e-mail, online and, in some cases, through home visits or at health centres. Citizens Advice is committed to providing a free, independent, confidential and impartial (unprejudiced) service which gives empowerment to individuals to obtain justice. In the UK it deals with about six million new problems each year.

The Samaritans

Some people get so distressed about their problems that they are prepared to take desperate measures to solve them and some even attempt to end their lives. Statistics for England and Wales show that over 4,000 people commit suicide each year, although many more attempt to take their own lives. The number has been falling for the past 30 years, thanks in part to the work of the Samaritans (see the Samaritans case study).

B *Samaritans provide a listening ear*

Samaritans

In 1953, a Church of England vicar, Chad Varah, set up an organisation called the Samaritans (the name comes from the Parable of the Good Samaritan, Luke 10:25–37). At that time, in London, there was an average of three suicides a day and Chad Varah wanted to do something to persuade those who were contemplating taking their own lives to think again. Although the organisation is not a religious one, it recognises the sanctity or value of human life. Now there are over 200 branches of the Samaritans in the UK, and over 17,000 trained volunteers operate a 24-hour, seven-day-a-week telephone answering service on 365 days of the year, where the volunteers listen to callers' problems. Other work includes operating a drop-in service for face-to-face discussion, a text service, confidential e-mail support and research into suicide and emotional health issues. The service offered is not counselling or advice but the provision of a listening ear and an opportunity to talk through problems anonymously. The aim is to help people share their distress, rather than feel despondent and suicidal.

Case study

Extension activity

2 Read the Bible story of the Good Samaritan (Luke 10: 25–37) and suggest why the Samaritans organisation was named after this parable.

AQA Examiner's tip

Be able to explain why the Citizens Advice service and Samaritans make an important contribution to UK society.

Discussion activity

With a partner, in a small group or as a whole class, discuss whether you think the Samaritans would be more or less effective if they extended the service from just providing a listening ear to giving advice to their callers.

Activities

1 Explain briefly what is meant by 'justice' and 'empowerment'.

2 Explain how the Citizens Advice service helps to give citizens justice and empowerment.

3 'Religious believers ought to do voluntary work for either Citizens Advice or the Samaritans.' What do you think? Explain your opinion.

Summary

You should now be able to describe the work and explain the importance of both the Citizens Advice service and the Samaritans.

6.6 Pressure groups

What is a pressure group?

Pressure groups may be involved in local, national or international issues. For example, the proposed closing of a residential home for the elderly by a council, or the building of a dual carriageway through a quiet village, may upset local residents. As a result, the residents may get together, form a group and decide to put pressure on their local councillors to oppose and defeat the schemes. Concern about rising prices and the level of pensions may cause pensioners nationwide to lobby parliament for an increase in the state pension. On an international scale, many people are concerned about global warming, climate change and the protection of wildlife. So pressure groups have been formed to present their viewpoints on these issues to governments throughout the world and to organisations such as the United Nations. Many people support pressure groups as they force politicians and those in authority to take certain issues seriously. Others do not support such groups because they think too much pressure might result in the wrong decisions being made.

Pressure groups include groups such as the Campaign for Nuclear Disarmament (CND), the Electoral Reform Society (which would like to change the voting system), the National Farmers Union (which promotes farmers' interests), Friends of the Earth (which lobbies Parliament on environmental issues) and the Countryside Alliance (which tried to stop the ban on fox hunting).

> **Objectives**
>
> Know about the work of pressure groups including Abortion Right and the Society for the Protection of the Unborn Child.

> **Key terms**
>
> **Pressure group**: an organised collection of people who seek to influence political decisions or promote a particular issue.
>
> **Abortion**: the deliberate termination (ending) of a pregnancy, usually before the foetus is twenty-four weeks and viable.

A Symbol of the Campaign for Nuclear Disarmament (CND)

> **Research activity**
>
> Choose one of the pressure groups listed on this page and find out more about their work and aims by using the internet or a library. Record your findings.

If the issues are very controversial, the formation of a pressure group against an issue will sometimes result in another group being formed to support it, such as groups for and against **abortion** (see the case studies on page 129).

Chapter 6 Religion and human rights

Case studies

Abortion Rights

Abortion Rights is a national, pro-choice campaign organisation that believes that women should have control over their own bodies. This pressure group is campaigning to defend and extend women's rights and access to safe, legal abortion. They are opposed to any attempt to lower the abortion time limit, and state that most women believe that they should have the right to choose whether or not to continue with a pregnancy. The organisation was formed in 2003 when the National Abortion Campaign (NAC) and the Abortion Law Reform Association (ALRA) joined together. They do not approve of two doctors having to agree to women being allowed an abortion, and seek to persuade Members of Parliament (MPs) to change the law in favour of abortion on demand.

The Society for the Protection of Unborn Children (SPUC)

SPUC was founded in the 1960s to fight for the rights of the unborn child. The society supports the 1959 United Nations Declaration of the Rights of the Child, which says, 'the child, by reason of his physical and mental immaturity, needs special safeguards and care, including appropriate legal protection, before as well as after birth.' Its aims include promoting the understanding of the value of human life from the moment of conception, the defence of the unborn child and the welfare of the mothers during pregnancy. It acts as a pro-life pressure group on the government, when laws are being proposed concerning abortion, representing the rights of the unborn child. It monitors the voting records of MPs and Members of the European Parliament (MEPs) on abortion, embryo experimentation and euthanasia, and informs the public of the way politicians have voted. SPUC produces leaflets and education packs, and sends speakers to schools and public debates to promote its aims.

Although its constitution is not based on religion, many members of SPUC are religious believers. In particular, members include SPUC Roman Catholic and evangelical Christians, and there is a Muslim division of the society.

AQA Examiner's tip

Abortion Right and SPUC are two pressure groups named in the specification, so make sure you know about their work and aims.

Discussion activity

With a partner, in a small group or as a whole class, discuss the following statement: 'Pressure groups do more harm than good.' Make notes on the opinions given and the reasons for them.

Activities

1. Give three examples of pressure groups other than Abortion Right and SPUC.
2. Give an outline of the aims of Abortion Right and SPUC.
3. 'Religious believers have a responsibility to get more involved in local pressure groups.' What do you think? Explain your opinion.

Summary

You should now know about and be able to explain the work and aims of at least two pressure groups.

6.7 Forms of protest

Protest

People are able to make known their opposition to a proposal in many different ways. The law has not always taken into consideration all groups of people, including those who form an ethnic or religious minority. When this happens, these groups may consider that their minority rights have been ignored, resulting often in resentment and discontent. Muslims protested about the blasphemy laws because they only applied to Christianity, not the minority faiths.

With the exception of a few extremists, most people choose non-violent, peaceful, lawful methods when they wish to protest. These include:

- writing letters to those involved, including elected representatives (such as MPs) or to the press
- organising a petition and collecting signatures
- persuading organisations to support them
- organising a march with banners, badges and posters
- involving the local media, including radio and television
- organising a deputation to a decision-making organisation, demonstrating or lobbying Parliament
- producing leaflets and flyers
- organising a public meeting or a sit-in
- setting up a website and e-mailing friends
- asking a trade union to organise a day of action or a strike.

In addition, religious believers might:

- pray about the situation, both in private and in public worship
- discuss the issue in faith groups and with religious leaders
- use passive resistance (peaceful non-cooperation)
- organise a religious parade.

The Universal Declaration of Human Rights (UDHR) allows the above actions. For example:

The Universal Declaration of Human Rights, 1948

Article 19 Everyone has the right to freedom of opinion and expression; this right includes freedom to hold opinions without interference and to seek, receive and impart information and ideas through any media and regardless of frontiers.

Article 20 Everyone has the right to freedom of peaceful assembly and association.

Objectives

Understand different ways people may protest.

Key terms

Minority: a small group differing from others.

Minority rights: the rights of a racial, ethnic, religious, linguistic or sexual minority group in a community.

Protest: a statement or action as a reaction to events or situations. Usually it is against something, although occasionally it can be in support.

A *Protest march*

links

Refer back to page 122 to remind yourself of the UDHR.

Chapter 6   Religion and human rights   131

B The organisation Greenpeace actively campaigns to protect the environment

Greenpeace – an environmental pressure group

Greenpeace was founded in Canada in 1971 and was originally called the Greenpeace Foundation. Its original aim was to oppose nuclear tests by the USA in Amchitka, Alaska. Greenpeace volunteers and journalists sailed into the area to try to stop the underground nuclear tests. Since then, the organisation has expanded to conduct worldwide, non-violent campaigns to protect the environment. In particular, Greenpeace has been actively involved in:

- promoting clean, renewable and efficient energy as an answer to climate change
- seeking to end the destruction of important forests
- campaigning to protect the oceans from radioactive and industrial waste
- trying to prevent commercial whale fishing and large-scale driftnet fishing
- protesting to ban the testing of nuclear weapons
- campaigning to protect mineral resources in Antarctica
- preventing the release of genetically-modified organisms into the environment
- seeking to eliminate persistent, toxic chemicals from being used in the world.

Greenpeace promotes its views by using the media to publicise the activities of its volunteers, who turn up where controversial actions are being planned and use non-violent methods to try to stop the environment from being damaged.

Case study

Extension activity

On the Greenpeace website research the campaigns it is currently involved in and the methods it is using to promote its views.

AQA Examiner's tip

Be able to identity different methods of protest and the appropriateness of each for a religious believer.

Discussion activity

With a partner, in a small group or as a whole class, discuss the effectiveness of different methods used in protesting. List, in order of priority, which you might use if you wished to promote an issue affecting your community. Give reasons for your opinion.

Activities

1. Explain what people mean when they talk about 'minority rights'.

2. Describe the aims of Greenpeace.

3. 'The best method of protesting is to attract lots of publicity.' What do you think? Explain your opinion.

Summary

You should now be able to write about different forms of protest as a means of publicising issues and protecting minority and human rights. You should also know about and understand the work of a protest group.

6.8 Religions and protest

Religions as pressure groups

Religious believers are often involved in protesting against what they see as injustice, or if they believe Article 18 of the Universal Declaration of Human Rights is being broken: 'Everyone has the right to freedom of thought, conscience and religion.' In Britain, for example, Christians in the 19th century campaigned for free education for young people, fought to abolish slavery and child labour and, in more recent times, some Christians have protested against abortion, the use of human embryos for research and human cloning, and activities that contribute to global warming. This is because Christians believe in the sanctity of human life and they follow the Bible teaching, 'Love your neighbour as yourself' (Mark 12:31).

The campaigning aspect of religions, which are determined to promote justice, means they are pressure groups in their own right. The Dalai Lama, a Buddhist leader, has favoured peaceful demonstrations. As a result, he was awarded the Nobel Peace Prize in 1989.

> The (Nobel) Committee wants to emphasise the fact that the Dalai Lama in his struggle for the liberation of Tibet consistently has opposed the use of violence. He has instead advocated peaceful solutions based upon tolerance and mutual respect in order to preserve the historical and cultural heritage of his people.
>
> *Nobel Committee*

With exception of a few extremists, most religious people choose peaceful methods when they wish to protest. Many support passive resistance because it uses non-violent methods to make the authorities take notice.

Most religious believers would not use violence as a means of protest. Throughout history, however, religious extremists have committed acts of violence and terrorism in pursuit of their aims.

Religions and human rights

Some religions have their own set of human rights. For example, Islam is based on the idea that 'Truly, God loves those who are just' (Qur'an 49:9). Following the Islamic Declaration of Human Rights 1981, the Cairo Declaration of Human Rights (CDHRI) was adopted in 1990 by 45 foreign ministers of the Organisation of the Islamic Conference, with the aim of serving as guidance to Muslims concerning human rights. Some religions have specific organisations designed to promote human rights. For example, the Hindu Human Rights (HHR) organisation is based in the UK and its stated aim is to educate people about the human rights of Hindus and to campaign against human rights abuses.

Objectives

Investigate religious responses to protest, pressure groups and human rights.

A A protest by Muslims in London

links

Remind yourself of peaceful methods of protest by re-reading pages 130–131. There is more about passive resistance in this chapter on pages 136–137.

AQA Examiner's tip

Be able to explain the involvement of the religion(s) you are studying in promoting human rights.

Chapter 6 Religion and human rights 133

> **Beliefs and teachings**
>
> This is the sum of duty: do not do to others what would cause pain if done to you.
>
> *Mahabharata 5:1517*

The Jews remember the horror of the Holocaust when six million Jewish people were murdered. In order to uphold human and minority rights, and help ensure that such a tragedy does not happen again, they promote the Holocaust Memorial Day, an international event that is held annually on 27 January.

Within Christianity, there is the organisation Christian Solidarity International. It was set up in Switzerland in 1977 to support persecuted Christians. The founder, Rev. Hans Stuckelberger, believed that every human being should have the right to choose his or her faith and to practise it as stated in Article 18 of the UDHR. The CSI is based on the principle that if one Christian suffers, all other Christians are affected:

> **Beliefs and teachings**
>
> If one part suffers, every part suffers with it.
>
> *1 Corinthians 12:26*

In 1993, the Parliament of the World's Religions met in Chicago and drew up an agreement concerning what the leaders of the different religions saw as common ground and areas where they could work together. Actions agreed included working for peace, protecting the environment and promoting the idea that human life should be treated with dignity. The Golden Rule of treating others as you wish to be treated was seen as a common thread through all the religions, along with the understanding that decisions, actions and failures to act have consequences.

B *Campaigning against corporate greed*

Research activity

Use the internet to find more about one of the following: Buddhist protest in Tibet, Christian Solidarity International, the CDHRI, the Hindu Human Rights or the Holocaust Memorial Day.

links

Find the rules about serving others (golden rules) for each religion on pages 68–69.

Discussion activity

With a partner, in a small group or as a whole class, discuss what 'religious rights' you think believers should have. Make notes on the opinions given and the reasons for them.

Activities

1. Give some examples of protests made by religious believers.

2. Explain how and why religious believers promote human rights.

3. 'Faith groups are the most important pressure groups.' What do you think? Explain your opinion.

Summary

You should now be able to explain religious attitudes and responses to methods of protest, pressure groups and the protection of human rights.

6.9 Religious protests and support for non-religious campaigning organisations

Religious protests

Religious believers often protest against those who make fun of their religion or who disrespect something they feel is sacred. Most teachings of the major religions encourage peaceful protest, but sometimes their followers do resort to violence. This is particularly the case when they believe that the sacredness of their faith and their religious rights are under attack, or that people of their faith are being encouraged to leave and join a different religion.

Buddhism

In Seoul, South Korea, in 2008, around 60,000 Buddhists took part in a rally to protest at alleged religious favouritism by President Lee Myung-bak and his government. President Lee had appointed mainly Christians to his cabinet, which the Buddhists regarded as unfair.

Christianity

Many Christians protested when an American play was performed in Britain, portraying Jesus as a hard-drinking homosexual. The play showed Jesus being crucified for being the King of the gays, after being betrayed by his lover Judas. This was seen as an insult to Jesus whom Christians believe to be the Son of God and 'the way, the truth and the life' (John 14:6).

Islam

Muslims became furious when cartoons of Muhammad were published in a Danish newspaper. It is illegal under Shari'ah Law to create pictures of Allah or the prophet Muhammad, but the insult was made worse because one of the images showed Muhammad wearing a turban shaped like a bomb. Muslims all over the world joined demonstrations against these cartoons. In 2005, many Muslims rioted because it was reported that prisoners at Guantánamo, in the USA, were being humiliated and forced to watch copies of the Qur'an being torn up by American soldiers.

Judaism

Jews protested when a new theme park, called the 'Holy Land Experience', was opened in Orlando. Publicity suggested that the multi-million dollar theme park was a living, biblical museum that would transport people through the pages of the Old and New Testaments. Jewish leaders were concerned that it trivialised sacred religious teachings with its cement camel prints and cafés offering 'Goliath burgers'.

Objectives

Find out about religious protests.

Investigate the work of Amnesty International and understand why many believers join such organisations.

Key terms

Amnesty: a pardon for crimes committed (usually against the state).

Beliefs and teachings

The person who struggles so that Allah's word is supreme is the one serving Allah's cause.

Hadith

A Cartoons can be controversial

Sikhism

Around 400 Sikhs protested in Birmingham over a play which they believed was insulting to the Sikh community. The play showed sexual abuse and murder, and was set in a Sikh gurdwara. The demonstrators were so incensed that they broke windows of the theatre, smashed some equipment and destroyed the foyer door. Three police officers were injured while trying to maintain peace and order.

Religious support for campaigning organisations

Despite the Universal Declaration of Human Rights and other human rights acts, religious persecution occurs in many countries. Minority religious group members may suffer from the destruction of their property, from being physically attacked or being unjustly imprisoned. Others lose their freedom for political reasons. Many religious believers join non-religious organisations, like **Amnesty** International (see the case study below). These are seen as independent organisations. Many people believe that they are more likely to be successful in helping in such situations. They also think that the more allies there are in fighting a cause, the higher the chances of success. Organisations that work to help the underprivileged, or to reduce suffering, are likely to be supported by religious believers because it is considered that they are doing good and supporting human rights.

B *Inside a Sikh gurdwara*

Case study

Amnesty International

Amnesty International was founded in Britain in 1961 to promote human rights wherever justice, fairness, freedom and truth are being denied. In 1977, it won the Nobel Peace Prize for its campaign against torture, and the UN Human Rights Prize in 1978. Ordinary people campaign for the release of people who have been imprisoned solely because their political, religious or ethical beliefs are in opposition to those held by the regime of the country in which they live. Amnesty International has been successful in persuading governments to change unfair laws and practices, and to respect human rights.

Discussion activity

With a partner, in a small group or as a whole class, discuss whether you agree with the following statement:

'Religious believers are too sensitive about any criticism of their religion.'

Make notes on the opinions given and the reasons for them.

Activities

1. Give some examples of incidents where religious believers have protested.

2. Explain why religious believers might support non-religious organisations.

3. 'Amnesty International proves that ordinary people can make a difference.' What do you think? Explain your opinion.

AQA Examiner's tip

Be prepared to write about the work of an organisation such as Amnesty International.

Summary

You should now be able to write about some examples of protests by religious believers and why believers might support non-religious organisations, such as Amnesty International.

6.10 Religious campaigners who support human rights

Campaigning by organisations and individuals

Many organisations support human rights, including some set up by the government. These include the Commission for Racial Equality and the Equal Opportunities Commission. In Britain, laws have been introduced which help to protect young people from being exploited, such as rules about the number of hours young people can work. In some countries citizens have not been so fortunate and religious groups and individuals have worked to change unjust laws.

> **Objective**
> Find out about the work of religious groups and individuals who have supported human rights.

Case study

Mohandas Karamchand Gandhi (1869–1948)

Commonly known as Mahatma Gandhi, he became a major political and spiritual leader in India. As a Hindu, he believed in ahimsa (non-violence), but wanted to bring about change for Indian citizens. He led a movement based on peaceful mass civil disobedience, the aims of which included easing poverty, giving women more rights and building religious tolerance, but above all to ending British control of India.

Gandhi first used the tactic of non-violent civil disobedience while he was a lawyer in South Africa (1893–1915). There he helped the Indian community in its struggle for civil rights. Later, in India, he became the leader of the Indian National Congress (1921) and led the Dandi Salt March in 1930 against the salt tax which Britain had imposed. Gandhi was regularly imprisoned for his actions, both in South Africa and India. He was assassinated in 1948.

Regarded as the Father of India, a national holiday is held each year on 2nd October, the anniversary of his birthday.

A Image of Gandhi on 100 rupee note

Extension activity

Learn more about Gandhi's life by watching the film *Gandhi* (1982), starring Ben Kingsley. Make brief notes on why Gandhi behaved as he did.

Case studies

Martin Luther King, Jr (1929–68)

Baptist minister Martin Luther King became a leader of the civil rights movement which sought to gain equal rights for black people in the USA. He admired Mahatma Gandhi and also advocated peaceful methods to bring about change. His most famous speech ('I have a dream…') was an inspiration to millions. In it he said, 'I have a dream that my four little children will one day live in a nation where they will not be judged by the colour of their skin, but by the content of their character'. Martin Luther King was awarded the Nobel Peace Prize for his campaigning to end racial segregation and discrimination by using non-violent methods, but four years later, in 1968, he was assassinated.

> **Research activity**
> Use the internet to find out more about how individuals or religious groups, from the religion(s) you are studying, have campaigned for human rights.

Desmond Mpilo Tutu (born 1931)

Desmond Tutu opposed the apartheid regime in South Africa and fought for equal rights for the black majority. He was elected Archbishop of Cape Town and later of Johnannesburg. He became head of the Anglican Church of South Africa and he won the Nobel Peace Prize in 1984. Tutu supported economic sanctions by the international community against his country, and organised peace marches in Cape Town. He encouraged the crowds to chant, 'We will be free! All of us! Black and white together!', and apartheid ended in 1994.

Note: Apartheid was a policy in South Africa of radical segregation where whites were seperated from blacks, and given privileges.

Discussion activity

With a partner, in a small group or as a whole class, discuss whether you agree that peaceful methods of protest are more successful than violent ones in bringing about change. Make notes on the opinions given and the reasons for them.

Not only have individual religious believers campaigned for human rights, but also groups within the major religions have done so. Examples include:

- The Buddhism Tibetan Centre for Human Rights and Democracy (TCHRD) seeks to promote and protect human rights of the Tibetan people, both inside and outside Tibet.
- Christian Solidarity Worldwide is a human rights organisation which campaigns for religious freedom, helps those persecuted for their Christian beliefs and promotes religious liberty for all.
- The Hindu Human Rights organisation began in 2000 to highlight the plight of Hindus suffering persecution in Afghanistan, and supports all Hindus who face persecution.
- The British Muslim Human Rights Centre (BMHRC) was formed to promote the human rights of Muslims in the UK. It does this by being a pressure group on the government and ensuring that British laws do not penalise Muslims.
- The Jewish Forum for Justice and Human Rights (JFJHR) was formed in the UK to fight against anti-Semitism, to highlight the Israeli-Palestinian conflict and to support asylum seekers.
- The Sikh Human Rights Group (SHRG) was formed in 1984 because of the worsening human rights situation in North West India. Its work includes the promotion of minority rights.

B *There are many accounts of the horror of Auschwitz*

Activities

1. Describe the work of one religious believer who campaigned for human rights.
2. Describe and give reasons for the work of a religious group that supports human rights.
3. 'Religions should work together to achieve religious freedom.' What do you think? Explain your opinion.

Summary

You should now know about and be able to explain the work of at least one individual and one religious group that supports human rights.

AQA Examiner's tip

An exam question might ask you to write about a religious group or individual who has supported human rights.

Assessment guidance

6

Religion and human rights – summary

For the examination you should now be able to:

- ✔ explain religious attitudes towards the law and human rights
- ✔ explain and evaluate the impact of religion on the rights and responsibilities of people as citizens
- ✔ explain some of the human rights included in the Universal Declaration of Human Rights and the Human Rights Act
- ✔ explain the work of the Citizen's Advice service, ChildLine and Samaritans
- ✔ give examples of local, national and international human rights issues
- ✔ describe the work of pressure groups, including Amnesty International, Greenpeace, Abortion Right and the Society for the Protection of Unborn Children (SPUC)
- ✔ explain and evaluate different types of protest
- ✔ explain what is meant by 'minority rights'
- ✔ give religious responses to protest, pressure groups and human rights
- ✔ explain why religious believers may support non-religious organisations
- ✔ explain how and why religious individuals and groups support human rights.

Sample answer

1 Write an answer to the following exam question:

'The most important human right is to have the freedom to belong to whatever religion you choose, or to no religion at all.'

Do you agree? Give reasons for your answer, showing that you have thought about more than one point of view

(6 marks)

2 Read the following sample answer.

> It is important for those who live in a country where their chosen faith is a minority one to be able to worship without fear of harassment. Even though the Universal Declaration of Human Rights says this, in many countries there is still religious persecution. Religious believers feel very strongly about their faith and many are even prepared to die rather than change to another religion.

> To them their religion is the most important thing in life as it affects their afterlife and so is the most important human right. Atheists would not agree with this statement as they are not religious believers. Instead they might argue that the right to a fair trial is more important because without this right there would be no real justice.

3 With a partner, discuss the sample answer. Do you think that there are other things that the student could have included in the answer?

4 What mark (out of six) would you give this answer? (Look at the mark scheme in the Introduction on page 7 (AO2) before you attempt this.) What are the reasons for the mark you have given?

AQA Examination-style questions

1 Look at the photograph and answer the following questions.

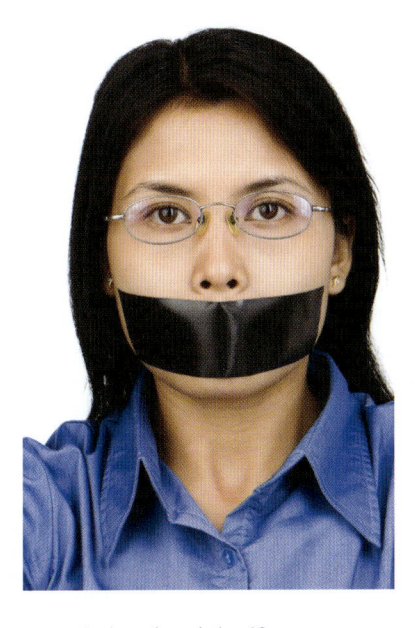

(a) What is meant by the term 'minority rights'? *(2 marks)*

(b) Describe briefly the aims of the Citizen's Advice service. *(3 marks)*

(c) 'Religious believers should always protest in a peaceful way.' What do you think? Give reasons for your opinion. *(3 marks)*

(d) Describe how an important religious believer campaigned to protect human rights. *(4 marks)*

(e) 'The worst human rights abuse is the persecution of religious believers.' Do you agree? Give reasons for your answer, showing that you have thought about more than one point of view. *(6 marks)*

AQA Examiner's tip

Remember when you are asked if you agree with a statement you must show what you think and the reasons why other people might take a different view. If your answer is one sided, you will only achieve a maximum of 4 marks. If you make no comment about religious belief or practice, you will achieve no more than 3 marks

Glossary

A

Abortion: the deliberate termination (ending) of a pregnancy, usually before the foetus is twenty-four weeks and viable.

Abuse: the harmful treatment of someone; the bad or wrong use of something.

Adultery: a sexual relationship between two people where at least one of them is married; sex outside marriage; an affair.

Age of consent: the age at which someone can legally agree to have a sexual relationship.

Amateur: a person who performs or takes part in an activity as a unpaid pastime, rather than as a profession.

Amnesty: a pardon for crimes committed (usually against the state).

Apartheid: a policy in South Africa of racial segregation where whites were separated from blacks, and given privileges.

Arranged marriage: a marriage arranged by parents.

Asylum seeker: a person who is seeking to be recognised as a refugee and requests permission to live in safety in another country.

B

Baisakhi: festival celebrating the formation of the Sikh Khalsa.

Binge drinking: consuming an excessive amount of alcohol in a short amount of time.

Blasphemy laws: the laws that prevent talk or behaviour that insults God or the gods.

Brotherhood: group that offers companionship, help and support to each other.

Business: a commercial or industrial firm. Sometimes business refers to the occupation, work or trade in which a person is engaged.

C

Career: way of making a living often in a profession.

Casino: a place where people play games of chance, such as roulette, blackjack and poker.

Celebrations: festivities to mark special occasions or events.

Celibacy: being unmarried; abstaining from sexual intercourse.

Chaplain: a priest, pastor, rabbi, imam or other member of the clergy who advises on moral, ethical and spiritual matters.

Charity: showing generosity towards others; an organisation that helps the needy.

Code of conduct: a set of principles and expectations that are considered binding on any person who is working for the company.

Commitment: 1. A promise to be faithful. 2. The state of being involved or obligated.

Conscience: the inner feeling of right or wrong that governs a person's actions.

Contraception: the artificial and chemical methods used to prevent pregnancy taking place.

Contract: 1. A formal agreement or legal bond. 2. An agreement concerning the responsibilities and conditions of work between employer and employee.

Covenant: an agreement.

Creative activities: activities that involve imagination and original thought, often in making things.

Culture: the customs and way of life of a group of people, including religious beliefs.

Custom: accepted or habitual practice, usually of long standing.

D

Differences: being different or unlike.

Disability: a physical incapacity caused by injury or disease.

Dishonesty: acts of lying, cheating or stealing.

Diversity: differences in customs, religious beliefs or opinion.

Divorce: the legal ending of a marriage.

E

Economy: the system by which the production, distribution and consumption of goods and services is organised in a country. The generation of wealth through business and industry.

Eid-Ul-Fitr: festival to mark the end of Ramadan.

Emigration: people leaving their home country to go and live in another country.

Employee: a person who works for another in return for wages.

Employer: a person or firm that employs (hires) workers.

Empowerment: the provision of the means to increase the spiritual, political, social or economic strength of individuals or communities.

Enterprise: a project or task that requires boldness or effort and a willingness to try new approaches or actions.

Exercise: physical activity intended to improve strength and fitness.

F

Fair competition: where the contestants have a more-or-less equal chance to win.

Fair play: the idea that everyone should behave reasonably, taking part in the spirit of the game or sport without using underhand tactics.

Fair wage: appropriate pay for the time, effort and skill given to the job.

Faith community: a group of people belonging to the same religion.

Family (The): a group of people who are related by blood, marriage or adoption.
Family commitments: the need to look after the family.
Festival: a religious celebration.
Freedom of choice: the idea that people can choose whatever they wish.

G
Gambling: playing games of chance for money.
Gamesmanship: tactics designed to distract or annoy opponents.

H
Health and safety: issues concerning the protection of employees.
Healthy living: living a life which is good for the body, both physically and mentally.
Heterosexual: a human who is sexually attracted only to the members of the opposite sex.
Homosexual: a human who is sexually attracted only to the members of the same sex.
Honesty: truthful. Not lying or cheating.
Human rights: the basic rights and freedoms to which all human beings should be entitled.
Human Rights Act: an act of parliament passed in 1998 which says that all organisations have a duty to protect the rights of all individuals in the UK.

I
Image: a characteristic of a person or group concerning style, manner of dress and how one is, or wishes to be, perceived by others.
Immigration: moving to another country to live there.
Inspiration: the stimulation of the mind that leads a person to do something creative.
Integration: different communities starting to live and work together and see each other as equals.
Interdependence: when two or more things depend on each other.

J
Justice: the bringing about of what is right or fair, according to the law, or the making up for what has been done wrong.

L
Law (The): a system of rules enforced by a country's legal system with consequences for those who break them.
Leadership: religious leaders who guide and help followers in matters concerning their faith.
Legal rights: rights that are laid down as an entitlement by law.
Leisure: free time. Time when an individual is not working.
Love: a feeling of deep affection, and in this case sexual attraction, for someone.

M
Marriage: a legal union between a man and a woman.
Marriage contract: a contract between a bride and groom.
Meaning of life: the purpose and significance of human existence.
Mementos: souvenirs.
Memorabilia: a collection of memorable things linked to a particular sport or person.
Minimum wage: the national minimum wage is the lowest hourly rate that it is legal for an employer to pay to employees or workers.
Minority: a small group differing from others.
Minority rights: the rights of a racial, ethnic, religious, linguistic or sexual minority group in a community.
Multicultural: consisting of many cultures, races and religions.
Multiple identities: several identities; for example, daughter, sports captain, Northerner, Briton.

N
Natural ability: an ability that is inherited and which is revealed by a quickness to learn, understand or acquire a skill.

P
Parenting: acting as a parent.
Peer pressure: the influence of those from a similar age group who encourage a person to change their attitude or behaviour to conform to the group's beliefs or actions, regarding, for example, fashion sense.
Performance-enhancing drugs: substances used by those involved in sport to improve their performance. This practice is illegal and is a form of cheating.
Personhood: the state or condition of being a person, especially having those qualities that confer distinct individuality and the ability to reason.
Pesach: festival celebrating the exodus of the Israelites from Egypt.
Physical dimension: that which can be experienced by the five senses and the physical body.
Pilgrimage: a physical journey to a special place. It can also be a person's inner spiritual journey.
Political correctness (PC): describes language, ideas, policies or behaviour seen as trying to minimise offence to racial, cultural or other identity groups.
Politics: the activities and affairs involved in managing a government, and the making of decisions that affect others' lives.
Pressure group: an organised collection of people who seek to influence political decisions or promote a particular issue.
Professional: a person who performs or takes part in an activity for payment.

Protest: a statement or action as a reaction to events or situations. Usually it is against something, although occasionally it can be in support.

R

Refugee: someone who flees from his or her home in search of safety and security.

Relaxation: the act of relaxing the body and/or mind in order to become less tense.

Religious voluntary organisation: a religious organisation that operates through voluntary contributions or voluntary labour.

Respect: an attitude of consideration and regard for the rights and feelings of others.

Responsibility: the legal or moral duty which a person has.

Rights: entitlements that all people should have.

S

Sabbath: a day of rest and worship.

Sacrament: an outward sign of a blessing or grace.

Sanctity of life: the idea that life is sacred because it is God-given.

Segregation: the separation of people according to their race or religion.

Self-worth: valuing yourself as a person.

Service: the work done by one person or group that benefits another. An act of help or assistance.

Sewa (Seva): selfless service: often refers to voluntary work or work offered to God (Hinduism, Sikhism).

Sex before marriage: sex between two single people.

Sex outside marriage: sex between two people where at least one of them is married.

Soul: the spiritual and immortal part of humans, which survives the death of the body. It is often thought to incorporate the inner awareness of each human being.

Spiritual dimension: that which relates to the soul or spirit in contrast to material or physical things.

Sponsorship: the provision of financial or material assistance by a private enterprise or business in return for publicity.

Sport: physical activity that is governed by a set of rules or customs; it is usually competitive.

Sportsmanship: an attitude that strives for fair play, courtesy towards teammates and opponents, decent behaviour and grace in losing.

State religion: the official religion of a country.

Stress: the mental or physical distress caused by pressure or difficult circumstances.

Stress relief: the reduction or removal of mental or physical distress.

Superstar: a widely acclaimed celebrity, such as a film star or sports star, who has great popular appeal.

Symbol: an object, image or action that represents something else.

T

Taxation: the method by which the government receives an income; for example, from income tax, Value Added Tax (VAT), inheritance tax.

Teamwork: working together for the benefit of the whole team.

Tithes: the giving of a tenth of your income to God.

Tolerance: the permitting of social, cultural and religious differences without protest, discrimination or interference.

Trade union: organisations that look after the interests of a group of workers.

Traditions: the handing down of customs from one generation to another.

U

Unemployment: the state of being without a job, especially involuntarily.

United Nations Declaration of Human Rights: document produced by the United Nations setting out the rights that all people should be entitled to.

V

Vocation: a career which the individual feels called to by God.

Voluntary organisation: an organisation that runs through voluntary contributions or voluntary labour.

Voluntary work: unpaid work, done willingly without expectation of a reward.

Vows: promises made by the couple to be faithful to each other.

W

Work: the physical or mental exertion in order to do, make or accomplish something.

Index

A
abortion 10, 14, 81, **128**, 129
Abortion Right 129
abuse 11, **124**, 125, 135
Adam and Eve 53, 101
adultery (affair) 12, 24–5, 26
age of consent **10**, 11
alcohol 36, 37, 112
amateur 48, **49**
amnesty **134**, 135
Anglican Church 13, 82–3
assessment guidance 6–7
asylum seekers 86, **87**
atheists 97

B
Baisakhi (Vaisakhi) **92**, 93
baptism 107, 109
Bar and Bat Mitzvah 108
Bhagavad Gita 101
binge drinking 36, **37**
blasphemy laws **82**, 83, 130
Brahman 101, 103, 107
brahmins 71, 107, 121
brotherhood 108, **109**
Buddha 33, 50, 90, 106
Buddhism 12, 87, 106
bullying 118
business 56, **57**

C
campaigning 12, 128, 133, 136–7
careers 54, **55**
casinos 36, **37**
caste 21, 71, 107, 110, 121
celebrations **76**
Chambers, Dwain 43
chaplain **46**
charity 67, 68, 69, 89
chastity 12, 21
cheating 42, 43, 62
ChildLine 125
children's rights 119, 124–5, 129
Christmas 90–1
Citizens Advice (CAB) 126–7
civil partnerships 10, 21
code of conduct 60, **61**
commitment 8, 9, **106**
confirmation 107
conscience **115**, 123
consciousness 100, 101
contraception 10, **14**, 15
contract 8, 9, 16, 17, 19, **62**
covenant 8, 9, 17, 103
creative activities 34
culture 78
custom 90, **110**, 111

D
Dalai Lama 54, 106, 132
death 25, 101
decision making 114–15
devas 98
dhamma 24, 48, 106, 112
differences 76
disability 48, **49**, 70
discrimination 65, 137
diversity **76**, 77, 79
divorce 24, 25, **26**–7
Diwali (Divali) 71, 91
dress, modest 13, 41, 105, 111
dress, religious 65, 110–11
drugs, performance–enhancing 42–3

E
economy **58**, 79
Eid-ul-Fitr 71, **92**
emigration 84
emotions 31, 98, 112
employee 61
employer 61
employment law 65
enterprise 56, 57
equality 48–9, 109
ethnic cleansing 118
European Union 75, 84
exercise 30, 31, 48

F
fair competition 40
fair wage 60, **61**, 63
faith communities **87**, 88–9
 identity in 106–9
family 8, 13, **22**, 23
family commitments **62**, 63
festival days 39, 70
festivals 71, **90**, 91, 93
films 34, 39, 98, 136
Five Pillars of Islam 59, 103
football 40, 44–5
forgiveness 24
freedom of choice **82**, 83
Fridays 71

G
gambling 36, 37

Gandhi, Mohandas Karamchand 121, 136
Genesis 9, 52
glossary 140–2
Greenpeace 131
guidance 114
gurdwaras 69, 109, 114, 135
Guru Granth Sahib 13, 19, 25, 67, 108, 113, 121

H
Hadith 27, 67, 113
Hajj 33, 103
health and safety 60, **61**
healthy living 32, **112**–13
heaven and hell 100, 101
Hebrews 79, 92
hejab (hijab) 111
heterosexual **10**
Hinduism 15, 103, 107
Holocaust 133
holy days 39, 52, 71
homosexuals (gay) **10**, 21
honesty 40
human life 96, 97, 99
human rights 63, 86, 118–19, **120**–5, 130
 abuses 118, 120, 125
 Act (HRA) 119, **122**, 123
 organisations 132, 133

I
identity 96–7, 106–9
image 104
imams 92, 108, 114
immigration **74**–5, 84–5
immortality 98, 100
inspiration 34
insults 120, 134, 135
integration 87
interdependence 115
interfaith groups 89
Islam 15, 108

J
Jesus 24, 26, 90, 102, 112
 parables 33, 67, 127
Jews 88, 133
Judaism 15, 108
judgement day 101, 103

K
karma 17, 24, 38, 59, 67, 101
Khalsa 92, 93

King, Martin Luther   136

L

laws   11, 83, 119, **120**
Laws of Manu   18, 24, 113
leadership   **106**, 107, 114
legal rights   **124**, 125
leisure   **32**–7, 46–7
Liddell, Eric   39
London   77
love   **12**, 20, 34
lust   13, 24, 25

M

Magna Carta   118
mark scheme   6–7
marriage   **8**, 9, 12, 16–17, 20, 21
marriage alternatives   21
marriage contract   **8**, 9, 19
meaning of life   **102**–3
meditation   23, 31
members of parliament   81, 119, 129
mementos   **44**
memorabilia   **44**
minimum wage   60, **62**, 63
minorities   **130**, 135
minority rights   **130**, 137
modest dress   13, 41, 105, 111
money, use of   40, 46
monks   21, 54, 110, 114
Morecambe Bay tragedy   60
Morocco factory tragedy   65
Moses   9, 53, 79, 80
mosques   34, 35, 77, 88
Muhammad   38, 80, 113, 134
multicultural   **74**–9
multiple identities   **115**
murder   118, 133, 135
music   34, 35, 78

N

National Health Service   85
natural ability   **34**, 35
nibbana   102
Nobel Peace Prize   54, 132, 136, 137

O

Olympics   39, 41, 43, 46, 49, 77
organisations, voluntary   68–9, 137

P

Paralympic Games   48–9
parenting   **22**
Paul, St   12, 23, 59, 70, 112, 120
peaceful protest   121, 130, 132
peer pressure   **104**

performance-enhancing drugs   **42**–3
persecution   86, 118, 135
personhood   **98**–9
Pesach   **92**–3
physical dimension   **96**
pilgrimage   **32**, 33, 44–5
political correctness (PC)   **87**
politics   77, **80**–1, 85
Popes   82, 107, 122
Powell, Asafa   43
prayer   56, 108
prejudice   79, 85
pressure groups   **128**–9, 131, 137
private sector   56, 58
professional   48, **49**
professions, unacceptable   55, 56
protest   **130**–1, 132–5
public sector   56, 58
Pullinger, Jackie   54

Q

Qur'an   13, 17, 25, 48, 80, 113, 120

R

rabbis   81, 108, 114
rebirth   14, 98, 100–3, 105
recession   58, 70
refugees   86, 87
relationships web   8
relaxation   **30**–1
religious voluntary organisations   **66**, 68–9, 137
re-marriage   26, 27
respect   **84**, 85, 120
responsibilities   **8**, 9, **118**, 119
rights   118
rights and responsibilities   60–3
Roman Catholic Church   13, 14, 26, 107
Rushdie, Salman   83

S

Sabbath   **38**, 39, 88
sacrament   17, 24
sacred writings   80, 112–13
Samaritans   66, 127
sanctity of human life   98, 132
schools   77, 88
segregation   **87**
self-worth   **104**
service   **66**
sewa (seva)   **66**, 67, 93
sex before marriage   **12**–13, 25
sex outside marriage   **12**, 24–5, 26
sexuality, human   10
Shabbat   23, 71
Shari'ah Law   41, 120, 134

Sikhism   15, 108–9
sin   24, 25, 102, 105
slavery   79, 118, 119
social class   21, 71, 107, 110, 121
soul   97, 100, 101, 104
spiritual dimension   **96**, 100–1
sponsorship   **46**, 47
sport   **38**–9, 40–3, 46–7, 77
sports fans   44–5, 46
state religion   **82**
stress   **30**, 112
stress relief   **30**, 31
Sunday   71
superstars   **46**, 49
symbols   45, 65, 93, **110**, 128

T

Talmud   15, 19, 36, 113
taxation   **58**–9
teamwork   **38**
temples   77, 87, 88
Ten Commandments   9, 80, 105
Tibet   54, 68, 75, 120, 132
tithes   **58**, 59
tolerance   **84**, 85
Torah   23, 25, 27, 71, 113, 121
trade unions   64
traditions   108, **109**
Tutu, Desmond Mpilo   137

U

UDHR   63, 130
unemployment   **70**
UNICEF   125
United Nations Declaration of Human Rights   122
untouchables   71, 121

V

violence   125, 132, 134
vocation   21, 54, **55**
voluntary organisations   **66**, 68–9, 126, 137
voluntary work   **66**–7
vows   **8**, 9

W

wages   46, 60, **61**, **62**, 63, 84
websites   5, 39, 82, 89
weddings   9, 18–19
Wesak   90
women in sports   41, 48
work   **52**–3, 63, 70–1, 79

X

xenophobia   79